Your TORONTO
BLUE JAYS
25th ANNIVERSARY
COLLECTION

CANADIAN CATALOGUING IN PUBLICATION DATA

Davis, Jefferson, 1962–
Your Toronto Blue Jays : The Blue Jays 25th anniversary collection
a year-by-year history

ISBN 1-55022-458-1

1. Toronto Blue Jays (Baseball team) – History.   I. Title.

GV875.T6D38 2001   796.357´64´09713541   C00-933259-6

Research by Peggy MacKenzie
Cover and text design by Tania Craan
Layout by Mary Bowness

Printed by AGMV

Distributed in Canada by
General Distribution Services,
325 Humber College Blvd.,
Etobicoke, ON, M9W 7C3

Published by ECW PRESS
2120 Queen Street East, Suite 200
Toronto, Ontario M4E 1E2
ecwpress.com

This book is set in Avenir and Concorde.

PRINTED AND BOUND IN CANADA

The publication of *Your Toronto Blue Jays* has been generously
supported by the Government of Canada through the
Book Publishing Industry Development Program.
Canadä

Your TORONTO BLUE JAYS 25th ANNIVERSARY COLLECTION

A YEAR-BY-YEAR HISTORY

JEFFERSON DAVIS

ECW Press

The author would like to thank Peggy, Ian and Julia for all their support and patience, Jean Bradshaw for her diligence, the splendid line-up at ECW (Jack David, Jen Hale, Tracey Millen, Mary Bowness, Amy Logan, and Erin Rozanski) for their excellence and enthusiasm, Tania Craan for her wizardry and the multifaceted cast of characters on and off the field who took Canada's baseball fans on a wild roller coaster ride over the past quarter century.

1977

54–107 .335 7th

The Season

The well documented snowstorm on opening day and the usual assortment of challenges facing a first year club failed to dampen the immense enthusiasm surrounding Toronto's entrance into the major leagues. From the 9–5 win over the Chicago White Sox at frigid Exhibition Stadium on April 7 through the humid "dog days" of August when much of novelty had worn off for the players, there were many exciting moments in that inaugural season.

The first edition of the Blue Jays was a blend of young hopefuls relishing a shot at the big leagues and a few veterans adding a new dimension to their careers by providing experience on the field and in the clubhouse. Their first pick in the expansion draft was Bob Bailor, the second player chosen overall after the Seattle Mariners called Ruppert Jones' name. Bailor went on to hit .310 as a rookie while pitcher Jerry Garvin, Toronto's second pick, started quickly and ended up with 10 wins. Other promising figures included pitchers Jim Clancy, Pete Vuckovich and Dave Lemanczyk, catcher Alan Ashby, first baseman Doug Ault and outfielder Alvis Woods. Bill Singer, Jerry Johnson, Otto Velez, Ron Fairly and Doug Rader were key veterans added to the mix.

Toronto surprised many opponents during their first month. Jerry Garvin started 5–0 and Otto Velez hit .442 in April. Lemanczyk became the team's best starter with 13 wins while Vuckovich was the most versatile pitcher after being thrust into the dual role of starter and closer. Fairly and Velez hit for power along with Roy Howell, acquired during the season. The team hit a respectable 100 home runs but often demonstrated a lack of experience at the plate and on the basepaths.

There were several noteworthy accomplishments by the team and individuals during the 1977 schedule. Bob Bailor's .310 batting average and Dave Lemanczyk's 13 wins were expansion team records. Alvis Woods tied a major league record by hitting a home run as a pinch hitter in his first major league plate appearance in the season opener. The team played the eventual World Series champion New York Yankees tough including a late-season 19–3 mauling of the Bronx Bombers in Yankee Stadium. When the schedule ended, the Jays finished $9^{1}/_{2}$ games behind their expansion cousins, the Seattle Mariners, but $13^{1}/_{2}$ games ahead of the New York Mets' all-time worst first-year performance in 1962.

STATISTICAL LEADERS

HOME RUNS	Ron Fairly 19
RBIs	Ron Fairly, Doug Ault 64
BATTING AVERAGE	Bob Bailor .310
STOLEN BASES	Bob Bailor 15
WINS	Dave Lemanczyk 13
ERA	Pete Vuckovich 3.47
STRIKEOUTS	Jerry Garvin 127
SAVES	Pete Vuckovich 8

HIGHS

◆ March 11 – The Jays defeat the New York Mets 3–1 in their first ever pre-season game.

◆ April 7 – Amid blowing snow, Toronto joins the major leagues in style by whipping the Chicago White Sox 9–5.

◆ June 27 – Yankees starter Ron Guidry carries a no-hitter into the fifth inning when he walks the bases full then gives up a grand slam to light-hitting infielder Hector Torres.

◆ August 9 – The Jays defeat Minnesota 6–2 in front of a home crowd that breaks the old expansion team first-year attendance record. Their record-setting grand total was 1,701,052.

◆ September 10 – Roy Howell drives in a franchise record 9 runs as the Jays pound the Yankees 19–3 giving them their worst beating at home in over 50 years. Howell registered 454 career RBIs in an eleven-year career that began with Texas in 1974 and ended in Milwaukee.

LOWS

◆ July 4 – The Boston Red Sox set a major league record by hitting seven solo home runs off Blue Jay pitching.

◆ The team finishes $45^1/_2$ games out of first and $9^1/_2$ in arrears of expansion cousins Seattle.

Some Odd Facts about the First Year

After a sparkling 5–0 start, Jerry Garvin becomes Toronto's hard-luck man by going 5–18 the rest of the way despite pitching fairly well.

The Jays outlast the eventual world champion Yankees 7–6 in an ugly game that saw light-hitting Hector Torres victimize Ron Guidry for a grand slam home run and Jerry Johnson strike out Thurman Munson to end the game on a pitch that was several feet off the plate.

While the Jays struggled on the road at Minnesota and Cleveland, they enjoyed a solid 4–4 record at Yankee Stadium against the eventual World Series champions.

Jerry Garvin

Veteran third baseman/DH Doug Rader hit the Jays' first extra inning home run on July 13 and the first inside-the-park home run on August 21.

Although utility outfielder Steve Bowling only played two major league seasons, he got hot late in the season and was named the Jays' player of the month for September.

The Jays win the season series against expansion mates Seattle by 6 games to 4. This didn't happen again until 1983.

Player Profile

Bob Bailor

Following the Seattle Mariners' selection of Ruppert Jones in the 1977 Expansion Draft, the Blue Jays opted for a young infielder from Connellsville, Pennsylvania – Bob Bailor. A prospect in the Baltimore Orioles' system, Bailor was known for his quick hands at the plate and swiftness on the basepaths.

There was barely a stir when Bailor's name was first mentioned in Toronto but, by the end of the first season, he was known across Canada. During that difficult year he hit .310 and stole 15 bases. Bailor's average was the highest ever by a player on a first year expansion team. He was selected Toronto's player- and rookie-of-the-year.

The sophomore jinx was not much of a factor in 1978 as Bailor's average was still a decent .264 and he drove in 52 runs. In 1979 his batting average was disappointing but he still managed 38 RBIs and stole 14 bases. During these trying years, Bailor was one of the few hitters and baserunners that caused the opposition any concern. He also showed a tough side on occasion and was often heard encouraging pitchers to throw inside or directly at hitters to make the point that the Jays would not be taken lightly.

Following the 1980 season, Bailor was traded to the New York Mets where he was a useful role player for three seasons. This was followed by two years with the L.A. Dodgers before he retired after having appeared in 955 games. He later returned to Toronto as a coach and was on hand along with fellow original Blue Jays Jim Clancy, Garth Iorg and Ernie Whitt when the team won its first division title in 1985.

Quotes

"There's an opportunity here in Toronto to put my mark on something and make it go. You always want to use your ingenuity, your mind and your development skills to try to put a club together and make it successful."

Pat Gillick after the Jays hired him away from the
Yankees in August 1976.

"The first thing I want to do is make everyone here aware of just how excited the people up in Toronto are about major league baseball arriving in their city."

Roy Hartsfield addressing the team for the first time as a group at the
start of spring training in Dunedin, Florida.

"I know I have a strong arm. In the minors, that was enough. But up here, if I throw it over the plate they hit it. They're not taking those good pitches and swinging at the bad ones."

Jim Clancy.

Otto Velez

April 9, 1977
WHITE SOX 5, BLUE JAYS 9

Chicago	ab	r	h	rbi	Toronto				
Garr, lf	5	2	3	0	Scott, rf	5	1	1	0
Bannister, ss	5	0	1	0	Torres, ss	2	1	1	0
Nyman, ph	1	0	0	0	Mason, ph	1	1	0	0
Norbr'k, ss	0	0	0	0	Ault, 1b	4	2	3	4
Orta, 2b	4	0	0	1	Velez, dh	4	1	2	0
Zisk, rf	6	2	4	2	G. W'ds, cf	5	1	1	0
Spencer, 1b	6	0	2	0	Bowling, rf	2	0	0	0
Gamble, dh	3	0	0	0	A. W'ds, dh	3	1	1	2
S'horn, 3b	5	0	2	1	Garcia, 2b	4	1	3	1
Lemon, cf	4	0	0	0	McKay, 3b	4	0	2	1
Downing, c	4	1	3	0	Cerone, c	4	0	2	0
Totals	43	5	15	4	Totals	38	9	16	8

Chicago	220	001	000 — 5	15	0
Toronto	112	120	02x — 9	16	3

E — Cerone, McKay, Scott. DP — Chicago (2). LOB — Chicago 19, Toronto 8. 2B — Garcia, Cerone, Scott, Zisk. HR — Ault (2), A. Woods, Zisk. SB — Garr, G. Woods. SF — Orta.

	IP	H	R	ER	BB	SO
Chicago						
Brett (L)	3	9	5	5	0	4
Barrios	3	3	2	2	3	1
Hamilton	1	3	2	2	0	1
Lagrow	1	1	0	0	0	1
Toronto						
Singer	$4^1/3$	11	4	3	3	5
Johnson (W)	$2^1/3$	2	1	1	3	1
Vuckovich	2	0	0	0	1	2

T — 3:22. A — 44,649.

1978

59–102 .356 7th

The Season

A five-win improvement did not prevent the Blue Jays from recording their second consecutive 100–loss season. Although a few positive signs were emerging, some key players were unable to duplicate their success of the previous season. Overall, the team was headed in the right direction but at a relatively slow pace.

The offence was bolstered by the addition of first baseman John Mayberry and designated hitter Rico Carty. Both veterans topped the 20 home run mark and provided veteran stability in the locker room. Mayberry went on to hit 255 career round trippers while Carty recorded 204 going back to his rookie year with the Milwaukee Braves in 1963. Bob Bailor continued to contribute by driving in 52 runs while rookie Rick Bosetti provided offensive and defensive spark in the outfield and third baseman Roy Howell drove in 61 runs. Veteran designated hitter Willie Horton arrived part way through the season to provide valuable batting tips to the Jays' youngsters. Unfortunately former hero Doug Ault was a non-factor and Alvis Woods' numbers slipped from the previous year.

On the mound starters Jim Clancy and Tom Underwood were the most consistent performers with the latter posting a misleading 6–14 record. Veterans Tom Murphy and Joe Coleman provided savvy in the bullpen before rookie Victor Cruz burst on to the scene in mid-season. On the downside Dave Lemanczyk slipped badly with a 4–14 record and right-hander Jesse Jefferson continued to tantalize with flashes of brilliance yet general inconsistency.

There were some memorable efforts along the way in the second season. Less than a month into the schedule the team recorded its first-ever triple play – Clancy started it by catching a sacrifice bunt by Junior Moore, then relaying to John Mayberry at first to double-up Ron Blomberg. Mayberry then threw to Luis Gomez to triple Lamar Johnson at second base. From May 9–16, the club recorded its most dominant homestand by winning 10 of 11 games versus Oakland, Seattle and California. On June 26, the Jays set a club record with 24 runs during a rout of the Baltimore Orioles. Included in this massacre was the third two-home run performance in a little over a month by John Mayberry. In a move that would yield many future dividends, management converted minor league outfielder Dave Stieb to a pitcher.

STATISTICAL LEADERS

HOME RUNS	John Mayberry 22
RBIs	John Mayberry 70
BATTING AVERAGE	Rico Carty .284
STOLEN BASES	Rick Bosetti 6
WINS	Jim Clancy 10
ERA	Victor Cruz 1.71
STRIKEOUTS	Tom Underwood 140
SAVES	Victor Cruz 9

HIGHS

◆ May 23, 1978 – Jesse Jefferson pitches a 12-inning complete game in a 2–1 victory over the Boston Red Sox and future Toronto manager Tim Johnson scores the winning run.

◆ June 26 – the Jays trounce the Baltimore Orioles 24–10 in the highest scoring game in franchise history. Eighteen-year-old Brian Milner slaps three hits and the O's are forced to deploy catcher Elrod Hendricks to give their beleagured pitching staff a break.

◆ June 29 – The Jays and Expos play the first Pearson Cup game at Olympic Stadium. Canadian pitcher Bill Atkinson jars the ball loose from catcher Alan Ashby to score the winning run in a 5–4 Montreal win.

◆ Rookie reliever Victor Cruz emerges in mid-season as an exciting new closer.

◆ First-year centerfielder Rick Bosetti drives in 42 runs and earns league-wide respect for his 17 assists.

LOWS

◆ Inaugural game hero Doug Ault drives in only seven runs and records a mere 104 at bats.

◆ 1977 Pitcher of the Year Dave Lemanczyk records a dismal 4–14 record and a 6.26 ERA.

◆ August 15 – After winning 6 out of 7 games, the Jays' clubhouse is stunned by the trading of popular Rico Carty to Oakland and promptly goes on a six-game winless streak.

Pitchers with the Most Career Wins When They Joined the Blue Jays

1. Phil Niekro 318

Veteran knuckleballer Phil Niekro was acquired by the Jays in 1987 with the hope that he would solidify the starting rotation as the fourth or fifth starter. He pitched reasonably well in his first start but in the next two the fatigue of nearly 24 years in the big leagues showed and he was released to make room for newly acquired Mike Flanagan.

2. Jack Morris 216

Morris was signed as a free agent prior to the 1992 season to provide quality starting pitching and a winning attitude from his stellar career in Detroit and Minnesota. That first year he became the Jays' initial 20–game winner and helped the club capture its first World Series. He tailed off in 1993 then spent one year in Cleveland before retiring.

3. Roger Clemens 192

Toronto made the biggest splash in the free agent market in 1997 by luring Red Sox ace Roger Clemens out of Boston. During his two years in Toronto he recorded consecutive 20–win seasons and Cy Young Awards.

4. Frank Viola 175

At spring training prior to the 1996 season Toronto gave veteran left-hander Frank Viola a look. He made the team but was released after posting a 1–3 record in six starts. Viola starred with the Minnesota Twins earlier in his career and helped that franchise win its first World Series title in 1987.

5. John Candelaria 174

A star for many years with the Pittsburgh Pirates in the 1970s, Candelaria pitched briefly for the Jays in relief during the 1990 season. During his 19 major league seasons he topped the 15–win mark three times.

6. Dave Stewart 146
Stewart was added to the Jays' starting rotation in 1993 to help replace the departed Jimmy Key. He responded with 12 wins and clubhouse leadership that helped Toronto repeat as World Series winners. After working on the executive and coaching staffs in Oakland and San Diego, Stewart returned to Toronto as Assistant General Manager, Director of Player Personnel and interim pitching coach.

7. Danny Darwin 146
Equally adept at starting and relieving, Darwin was added to the Jays as the fourth or fifth man in the rotation in 1995. He did not fare well and was let go after a dismal 1–8 record and 7.62 ERA in 13 appearances. Darwin's best year was a 15-win performance for Boston in 1993.

8. Joe Coleman 140
Toronto picked up the veteran Coleman in 1978 after he shifted to the role of a relief pitcher and he responded with two wins and some solid work. As a starter, he won 86 games for Detroit between 1971 and 1975 including two 20–win seasons.

9. Mike Flanagan 139
A crafty left-hander with excellent control, Flanagan was acquired by the Jays as they entered the stretch drive of the 1987 pennant race. Although the club faltered, he pitched well and went on to win 13 games for Toronto the next season. Flanagan was best known for winning 23 games and the AL Cy Young Award while pitching for Baltimore in 1979.

10. Bill Singer 119
Singer was the Jays' opening day pitcher when they debuted in the American League on April 7, 1977. He was unable to stay healthy, however, and finished the year with a 2–8 mark and 6.79 ERA. Singer's best years came in the late 1960s and early 70s when he won 20 games for the L.A. Dodgers in 1969 and the California Angels in 1973.

Player Profile

Jim Clancy

A soft-spoken righthander known as "Clam," who stood 6'4", Clancy was a workhorse on the Jays starting staff for twelve seasons. Plucked from the Texas Rangers in the 1977 Expansion Draft, the affable native of Chicago, Illinois, was a star quarterback in high school before a broken collarbone turned him off football. Clancy was one of only three original Blue Jays on hand for the team's first division title in 1985. In all, he won 128 games in a Toronto uniform, many of which came during the franchise's early years of struggle. His trademark pitches were a 90–mile-an-hour fastball and a nasty breaking slider.

Clancy's value came to the fore in 1978 when he emerged as the club's most reliable starter. His 10–12 record and 194 innings pitched saved the Jays from complete disaster since Dave Lemanczyk and Jerry Garvin's combined win total dropped from 23 to 8. Clancy went on to record seven more seasons of at least ten wins including a personal high of 16 in 1982. His reliability and endurance were partly attributable to his easy going personality and positive outlook.

The burly right-hander flirted with history on September 28, 1982, when he lost a bid for a no-hitter during a 3–0 win over the Minnesota Twins. He left the Jays after the 1988 season trailing only Dave Stieb in career wins. The laidback right-hander was the first Toronto pitcher to pitch in 100 games and work 1,000 innings. He finished his major league days as a part-time starter with Houston then Atlanta where he won game three of the 1991 World Series. Clam was best remembered as a fixture on the Jays' starting rotation for many years. After retiring, he returned to the Jays' spring training home in Dunedin, Florida, where he purchased a condo overlooking the Gulf of Mexico and played round after round of golf.

Quotes

"Heat doesn't bother me. Cold doesn't bother me. Wind doesn't bother me. The only thing that bothers me is spiders. There weren't any spiders out there, so I was alright."

Dave Lemanczyk's eccentric view
of the secret to his success.

"I think I'll always be a good hitter."

Rico Carty after hitting a single and double during
his first game with the Blue Jays.

June 26, 1978

BLUE JAYS 24, ORIOLES 10

Baltimore	ab	r	h	rbi	Toronto				
Garcia ss	5	0	1	2	Upshaw lf	5	1	2	1
Dauer 3b	4	2	2	1	Bailor cf	5	4	2	1
Murray 1b	5	0	2	1	Howell 3b	5	3	2	4
S'g'ton rf	4	0	0	0	Carty dh	6	2	2	3
May dh	5	2	4	3	Velez rf	3	4	3	2
Mora lf	5	0	0	0	Ault 1b	1	1	1	0
xLopez cf	4	1	1	0	M'b'ry 1b	5	3	3	7
Smith 2b	4	2	1	2	McKay 2b	5	1	3	3
D'psey c	2	2	1	0	Gomez ss	2	1	1	1
Johnson ss	4	1	2	0	Milner c	5	3	3	2
Ashby c	1	0	0	0					
Totals	43	10	14	9	Totals	47	24	24	24

x — Awarded first base on catcher's interference.

Baltimore	101	310	031	— 10	12	0
Toronto	094	650	00x	— 24	24	1

E — Milner. DP — Baltimore 1, Toronto 1. LOB — Baltimore 7, Toronto 8. 2b — Murray, Bailor, Velez 2, McKay 2, May, Howell, Garcia, Mayberry. 3b — Howell, Milner. HRs — Mayberry 2 (12), May 2 (15), Smith (4). SF — Upshaw.

	IP	H	R	ER	BB	SO
Baltimore						
Flanagan (L, 11-5)	1	6	6	6	1	1
Kerrigan	1 1/3	9	7	7	0	0
T. Martinez	1 2/3	5	6	6	2	3
Harlow	2/3	2	5	5	4	1
Hendricks	2 1/3	1	0	0	1	0
Stanhouse	1	1	0	0	0	1
Toronto						
U'derw'd (W, 4-7)	5	6	6	5	4	0
Murphy	4	6	4	4	1	0

Flanagan pitched to 6 batters in 2nd.

WP — Harlow, Murphy. PB — Milner 2. T — 2:58. A — 16,184.

Victor Cruz

1979

53–109 .327 7th

The Season

The Jays experienced an extremely disappointing season in 1979. Rather than continue to move towards respectability, the team lost a franchise record 109 games and appeared to be regressing in a number of areas. The problems were evident early as the team went through its worst-ever homestand losing 10 of 12 games between May 18 and 31. On August 25, 1979, Toronto bottomed out during a humiliating 24–2 loss at the hands of the powerful California Angels.

The most glaring deficiency was the pitching corps which posted a league-worst 4.82 ERA. The best starter was Tom Underwood whose luck worsened with a unjust 9–16 mark despite a respectable 3.69 ERA in 227 innings of work. At one point the snakebit lefty lost 13 straight decisions even though he often pitched very well. The overall performances off the mound were poor however. Jim Clancy's breakthrough season was followed by a disheartening 2–7 performance, Jesse Jefferson was a poor 2–10, newcomer Mark Lemongello flopped with a 1–9 record and Dave Lemanczyk could only muster 8 victories. There were glimmers of hope in the form of rookie Dave Stieb's eight wins, Phil Huffman's 173 innings pitched and veteran Tom Buskey's yeoman service out of the bullpen.

Offensively John Mayberry and Roy Howell were the key figures, Rick Bosetti continued to excel with 65 RBIs and 619 at bats and Rick Cerone drove in 61 runs after inheriting the starting catcher's job from the traded Alan Ashby. In addition, first-year shortstop Alfredo Griffin hit .287, stole 21 bases and led the Jays with 81 runs. His fine effort earned him a share of the American League rookie-of-the-year award with Minnesota's John Castino. On the other hand Toronto's woes in 1979 could not be pinned solely on the pitchers. The club's high hopes for second baseman Danny Ainge proved unfounded, Bob Bailor slipped badly to a .229 batting average, Rico Carty produced only 12 home runs and Otto Velez was restricted to 99 games. The last three were at the tail end of their major league careers while Brigham Young University star Ainge bacame a success in the National Basketball Association as a player and a coach.

STATISTICAL LEADERS

HOME RUNS	John Mayberry 21
RBIs	John Mayberry 74
BATTING AVERAGE	Otto Velez .288
STOLEN BASES	Alfredo Griffin 21
WINS	Tom Underwood 9
ERA	Tom Buskey 3.43
STRIKEOUTS	Tom Underwood 127
SAVES	Tom Buskey 7

HIGHS

◆ Otto Velez becomes the first Blue Jay to be named the American League Player of the Week after hitting .500 and driving in 9 runs between July 23–29.

◆ August 26 – the Jays rebound on the field and emotionally from the previous day's massacre by pounding Angels' star Nolan Ryan in a 9–3 win.

◆ September 23 – Toronto announces that its three-year home attendance total of 4,695,288 represents a record for expansion teams.

◆ November 26 – Alfredo Griffin is selected the American League's co-Rookie-of-the-Year with John Castino of the Twins.

LOWS

◆ May 31 – Tom Underwood pitches another gem but loses 1–0 to his younger brother Pat, a rookie starter with the Detroit Tigers. This is a fitting end to a disasterous 2–10 homestand.

◆ August 25 – the Jays are forced to use back-up infielder Craig Kusick as a pitcher during the infamous 24-2 pounding at the hands of the California Angels.

Best Trades

November 1, 1979 — Tom Underwood, Rick Cerone and Ted Wilborn to the New York Yankees for Chris Chambliss, Paul Mirabella and Damaso Garcia

Underwood was a half-decent pitcher and Cerone played well at the beginning for the Yankees but the Jays acquired their future second baseman in Garcia. The youngster stepped immediately into the Toronto line-up and played seven years with the Jays where he became one of the best in the AL at his position.

Rance Mulliniks

March 25, 1982 — Phil Huffman to Kansas City for Rance Mulliniks

Huffman showed some promise as a rookie in 1979 but never pitched for the Royals while Mulliniks played a decade in Toronto where he was best known for his solid platoon with Garth Iorg at third base.

July 5, 1986 — Doyle Alexander to Atlanta for Duane Ward

Alexander wanted out of Toronto and was sporting a so-so 5–4 record when he was sent to the Braves for a young starter with a fastball in the high nineties. Ward eventually blossomed in the Jays' bullpen as Tom Henke's set-up man, and then the top closer in 1993 with a team record 45 saves before his career was cut short by arm miseries in 1994.

July 31, 1989 — Jeff Musselman, Tony Castillo and Mike Brady to the New York Mets for Mookie Wilson

The Jays were an improved club under new manager Cito Gaston but their ascent to the top of the division began in earnest during an August hot streak. The easygoing yet competitive Wilson was a major catalyst in this crucial month which propelled Toronto to its second division title.

December 5, 1990 — Tony Fernandez and Fred McGriff to San Diego for Joe Carter and Roberto Alomar

All four principals continued to play well after this deal but Alomar and Carter proved to be the on field additions that helped elevate Toronto to World Series winners. Carter added power and leadership while Alomar became one of the top second baseman of his era.

February 18, 1999 — Roger Clemens to the New York Yankees for David Wells, Graeme Lloyd and Homer Bush

Clemens pitched well for the Yankees but not as spectacularly as he did in Toronto and, for the most part, not as effectively as Wells. Boomer won 17 games in 1999 and reached the 20–win mark for the first time in 2000 when he was named the starting pitcher in the All-Star game. Bush enjoyed a solid year in 1999 then was hampered by injuries in 2000. He remained the Jays second baseman of the future with his combination of speed and hitting for average.

June 12, 1999 — Dan Plesac to Arizona for John Frascatore and Tony Batista

Plesac was a likeable individual near the end of his career whose experience was needed by the young Diamondbacks' pitching staff. Frascatore was inconsistent as a long reliever but Batista hit for average and power while replacing the injured Alex Gonzalez at shortstop in 1999. The next year he moved to third to replace the departed Tony Fernandez and earned selection to the American League squad at the All-Star Game. Plesac returned to the Jays as a free agent prior to the 2001 season.

Player Profile

Alfredo Griffin

A few eyebrows were raised when the Jays swung a deal in December 1978 that sent rookie sensation Victor Cruz to the Cleveland Indians for infielders Phil Lansford and Alfredo Griffin. Pat Gillick knew what he was doing as Cruz was essentially a one-year wonder while Griffin became one of the best young shortstops in the American League.

Born in Santo Domingo, Dominican Republic, Griffin started with the Cleveland Indians organization as a minor leaguer and reserve on the parent club. Following his trade to Toronto he became the team's starting shortstop and was one of the few bright lights in the dismal 1979 season. He hit .287 and stole 21 bases while earning a share of the American League Rookie-of-the-Year award with Minnesota's John Castino.

In his sophomore year he drove in 41 runs and led the AL with 15 triples. He was a fixture in the Jays' line-up during the early 1980s and took part in his first all-star game in 1984. Unfortunately Griffin was traded with Dave Collins in the Bill Caudill deal prior to the 1985 season and missed the franchise's first division title. Along with the emergence of Tony Fernandez, it was the selection of Manny Lee off the Houston Astros unprotected list five days before the trade that sealed the veteran shortstop's fate.

The popular infielder spent three years in Oakland and four with the L.A. Dodgers before returning to Toronto as a utility player in 1992. The club he rejoined was even stronger than the one he left in 1984. Griffin was able to retire in 1993 with two straight World Series rings, 527 career RBIs and 192 stolen bases.

Quotes

"Roy Hartsfield has never seen me play, not on an extended basis. Neither have Toronto fans."

Catcher Ernie Whitt venting his frustration at 1979 spring training.

"I'm hitting .300 with men on base. With nobody on I'm point something. When I come up with the winning run on, I just know I'm gonna get a hit. The other times, I don't know what it is."

Catcher Rick Cerone

"I was happy with what I did last year, but I was surprised to be Rookie-of-the-Year, because there were guys from the Yankees and Texas and these clubs had better years than the Blue Jays."

Alfredo Griffin looking back on the 1979 season.

August 27, 1979
ANGELS 3, BLUE JAYS 9

Angels	ab	r	h	rbi	Toronto				
Carew 1b	4	1	1	0	Griffin ss	2	0	0	0
L'f'rd 3b	4	1	1	0	Gomez ss	3	0	1	1
Ford rf	5	0	1	2	Cannon rf	5	0	0	0
Baylor lf	4	0	0	0	Howell 3b	3	0	0	0
Aikens dh	4	0	1	0	S'aita dh	3	1	1	0
Dow'ng c	2	0	0	0	May'y 1b	3	2	2	2
Grich 2b	3	1	1	0	Bosetti cf	3	2	1	0
R. M'er cf	4	0	2	1	Woods lf	1	3	1	0
A'dsn ss	3	0	0	0	Bailor rf	0	0	0	0
Thon ss	0	0	0	0	Cerone c	3	1	2	5
					Ainge 2b	4	0	0	0
Total	33	3	7	3	Total	30	9	8	8

California	001	000	200 — 3	7	0
Toronto	030	112	20x — 9	8	0

DP — California 2, Toronto 1. LOB — California 11, Toronto 6. 2B — Bosetti, Cerone, Woods, Ford. 3B — Grich. HR — Mayberry 2 (19), Cerone (5).

	IP	H	R	ER	BB	SO
California						
Ryan (L, 13-10)	5	6	5	5	5	1
Clear	1 2/3	2	4	4	3	2
Barlow	1 1/3	0	0	0	0	1
Toronto						
Edge (W, 2-1)	6 1/2	5	3	3	7	4
Buskey	2 2/3	2	0	0	1	2

HBP — By Clear (Bosetti). WP — Clear. PB — Downing. T — 2:29. A — 22,619.

Bobby Cox

1980

67–95 .414 7th

The Season

A light at the end of the tunnel appeared in the form of the 1980 season. Toronto avoided 100 losses for the first time and fielded its most competitive line-up to date. Under new manager Bobby Mattick the Jays performed more aggressively and with greater confidence. Although they were a far cry from playoff material, the team appeared to reach the next rung on the ladder in the competitive AL East. Much of the club's improvement was based on an injection of new blood in the form of Lloyd Moseby, Damaso Garcia, Barry Bonnell and Willie Upshaw. In an unexpected twist, veterans Jerry Garvin, Mike Willis and Alvis Woods rebounded with their most consistent seasons after being given a second chance by Mattick.

For the first time in four years opposing pitchers were required to be mindful of the Jays' bats. John Mayberry became the first Toronto player to reach the 30 home run plateau and five hitters reached double figures in round trippers. An off-season trade with the Yankees brought second baseman Damaso Garcia to Toronto and he responded by hitting .278 and playing excellent defence. Combined with Griffin at short, Howell at third and Mayberry at first, the Jays enjoyed a sound infield line-up for the first time. In the outfield Woods, Barry Bonnell and emerging star Lloyd Moseby compensated for the reduced production from Rick Bosetti. Overall the offence established new highs with 126 home runs and nearly 600 runs scored.

Toronto's starting pitching rotation was fairly stable throughout the season. Jim Clancy and Dave Steib won 13 and 12 games respectively while five starters topped 120 innings pitched. The weak link was the bullpen where newly acquired Joey McLaughlin was effective one day but horrid the next. Veterans Jerry Garvin, Mike Willis and Mike Barlow combined for 16 saves but the lack of a legitimate closer cost the team a few wins. Nonetheless the club's 4.19 ERA was far superior to the numbers from the previous three seasons.

May 17, 1980
BLUE JAYS 1, A's 0

Oakland	ab	r	h	rbi	Toronto				
Henderson lf	4	0	0	0	Griffin ss	4	0	0	0
Murphy cf	4	0	0	0	Bosetti cf	3	0	1	0
Page dh	4	0	1	0	Woods lf	5	0	1	0
Revering 1b	4	0	0	0	Howell 3b	5	0	2	1
Gross 3b	4	0	0	0	Mayberry 1b	3	0	0	0
Armas rf	4	0	0	0	Upshaw dh	4	0	0	0
Newman c	4	0	1	0	Garcia 2b	4	0	0	0
Guerrero ss	4	0	1	0	Bonnell rf	4	0	0	0
Picciolo 2b	4	0	1	0	Whitt c	3	0	0	0
					Bailor ph	0	1	0	0
Totals	36	0	4	0	Totals	35	1	4	1

Two outs when winning run scored

Oakland	000	000	000	00 — 0 4	0
Toronto	000	000	000	01— 1 4	0

LOB — Oakland 8, Toronto 7. 2B — Newman, Woods. SB — Murphy, Gross. S — Page, Griffin.

	IP	H	R	ER	BB	SO
Oakland						
Norris (L, 5-1)	10²/₃	4	1	1	4	4
Toronto						
Jefferson (W, 2-1)	11	4	0	0	4	10

T — 2:52. A — 16,138.

STATISTICAL LEADERS

HOME RUNS	John Mayberry 30
RBIs	John Mayberry 82
BATTING AVERAGE	Alvis Woods .300
STOLEN BASES	Alfredo Griffin 18
WINS	Jim Clancy 13
ERA	Jerry Garvin 2.29
STRIKEOUTS	Jim Clancy 152
SAVES	Jerry Garvin 8

HIGHS

◆ During the Major League Rule 5 Draft, the Jays select outfield prospect George Bell from the Philadelphia Phillies' minor league system. Bell eventually became one of the top power hitters in the game and was chosen the MVP of the American League in 1987. (In the Rule 5 Draft, players with at least 3 years of professional experience, who are not protected on a team's major league roster, are available for selection by another team for cash – today $50,000. The individual drafted must remain with his new club for the full season or be offered back to his original organization for half the price.)

◆ May 4, 1980 – In a game against the Cleveland Indians Otto Velez becomes the first Toronto player to hit three home runs.

◆ May 16 – Jesse Jefferson outduels Oakland ace Mike Norris over eleven innings in a thrilling 1–0 encounter.

◆ May 19 – Jim Clancy pitches the Jays to a 7–2 win over the Red Sox giving the club a 19–13 record and moving them to within a 1/2 game of the first place Yankees.

◆ September 12 – The Blue Jays defeat Baltimore 7–5 to reach the 60-win mark for the first time.

LOWS

◆ After a promising rookie season, Bob Bailor's decline continued with a dismal .236 average and 16 RBIs.

◆ Acquired from the Yankees in the Damaso Garcia trade, Paul Mirabella disappoints as a starter with a 5–12 record.

Blue Jays Firsts

First Player To Lead Off a Game with a Home Run: Bob Bailor
On April 27, 1977, Bailor connected off Indians' starter Wayne Garland in a game at Cleveland Municipal Stadium.

First Game To Last at Least 15 Innings: August 28–29, 1980
The Twins defeated the Jays 7–5 in a game that lasted 15 innings but had to be completed on August 29 due to the curfew in place during the Canadian National Exhibition.

First Inside-The-Park Home Run: Doug Rader
Veteran Doug Rader made it all the way home on August 21, 1977, against Frank Tanana and the California Angels.

First Home Run in Extra Innings: Doug Rader
Rader connected off Chicago White Sox reliever Jack Kucek in the 11th inning on July 13, 1977.

First Blue Jay To Lead the League in Triples: Alfredo Griffin
In 1980 speedy shortstop Alfredo Griffin led the AL with 15 triples in a solid sophomore season.

First Blue Jay AL Rookie Pitcher of the Year: Mark Eichhorn

Mark Eichhorn

In 1986 Eichhorn's sidearm delivery and control baffled hitters as he finished with a stingy 1.72 ERA and 166 strikeouts in 157 innings.

First Inter-league Game: June 13, 1997
The Jays began their interleague schedule by dropping a 4–3 decision to the Philadelphia Phillies at Veterans Stadium. The crowd saved its loudest chorus of boos for Jays' outfielder and 1993 World Series hero Joe Carter.

Player Profile

John Mayberry

Big John Mayberry was the first marquee slugger acquired by the Blue Jays while he was still in his prime. He hit 143 home runs for the Kansas City Royals between 1972 and 1977 before joining Toronto. His power and consistency helped Mayberry become a fan favorite from 1978 to the early stages of the 1982 season.

Mayberry led the Jays with 22 home runs and 70 RBIs during their second season in 1978. That year he had a penchant for hitting two home runs in a game, accomplishing the feat three times in just over a month. The next year he was one of the few bright spots in a disappointing season as he drove in 74 runs even though he took part in 15 fewer games. In 1980 Mayberry enjoyed one of his finest years with 30 home runs and 82 RBI's as the Jays played much better under new manager Bobby Mattick.

Injuries and the emergence of Willie Upshaw at first base lessened Mayberry's playing time in 1981 and the first month of 1982. He was sent to the Yankees where he played his last 69 games before retiring. Mayberry hit 92 home runs for Toronto in a career that saw him register 255 round trippers in a fine 15-year tenure. He later returned to the Jays in the mid-1980s as the team's roving minor league hitting instructor. Two of his students at the time were future stars Fred McGriff and Cecil Fielder.

Quotes

"Don't be watching the ball to see if it stay in the ballpark! Throw strikes. Throw strikes."

Rico Carty reacting to Jesse Jefferson's pause while delivering pitches in spring training batting practice.

Red Sox manager Don Zimmer responding to the question of whether or not he was surprised by the Jays' strong start in April and May, "No sir, I ain't surprised at nothing that happens in baseball. They're out there to win and they're winning."

"It's confidence. It's someone telling you that you can do it instead of someone telling you that you can't do it."

Roy Howell reflecting on the team's improved fortunes under Bobby Mattick.

"It's a shame Norris had to lose a game like that. They should change the rules. If two pitchers are locked in a 0–0 tie after nine innings, they should both be given half a game in the win column."

Jays' third baseman Roy Howell after Jesse Jefferson outduelled the previously unbeaten Mike Norris of the A's 1–0 over 12 innings.

When asked about the Jays' lack of hitting, manager Bobby Mattick quipped, "I guess I better go to the market tomorrow morning and buy some."

"I told them it's a long winter when you close out the season by losing 11 in a row."

Bobby Mattick describing his speech to the players as they entered the last series of the year in Boston riding an 8-game losing streak.

1981

1st Half 16–42 .276 7th
2nd Half 21–27 .438 7th

The Season

During a year divided by a player's strike, the Jays were a split personality themselves. They began by playing their worst baseball since joining the major leagues but were rejuvenated by the clean slate presented to every team in the second half of the schedule. Even though the team finished in last place, Toronto stood only $7^{1}/_{2}$ games behind the Milwaukee Brewers when "Act II" of the regular season ended.

The team was led by two emerging impact players: Dave Stieb and Lloyd Moseby. Stieb's 11–10 record made him the first Toronto pitcher to finish a season with a winning record while Moseby finished as the team's co-leader with 43 RBIs. Jim Clancy and Luis Leal were mainstays on the starting rotation while Joey McLaughlin, Jerry Garvin and Roy Lee Jackson led the bullpen. Still, the team lacked a closer and Stieb was the only starter to pitch well consistently.

Toronto's key problem in 1981 was its anemic batting order. Moseby joined veterans John Mayberry and Otto Velez as the only legitimate power hitters on the Jays. Damaso Garcia suffered through a batting slump during the first half but was hitting at a torrid .375 pace before his season was ended by a broken wrist in August. Overall the club hit an embarrassing .226 and received only 36 RBIs from its designated hitters.

There was a silver lining to the black cloud that was 1981. Young prospects Jesse Barfield and George Bell proved they could play at the major league level and were expected to form a superb outfield with Moseby. Additionally, first baseman Willie Upshaw and catcher Ernie Whitt moved forward in their development and indicated that they would contribute more in the future.

May 16, 1981
Len Barker's Perfect Game
JAYS 0 at INDIANS 3

Toronto	ab	r	h	rbi	Cleveland	ab	r	h	rbi
Griffin ss	3	0	0	0	Manning cf	4	1	1	0
Moseby rf	3	0	0	0	Orta rf	4	1	3	1
Bell lf	3	0	0	0	Hargrove 1b	4	1	1	0
Mayberry 1b	3	0	0	0	Thornton dh	3	0	0	1
Upshaw dh	3	0	0	0	Hassey c	4	0	1	1
Garcia 2b	3	0	0	0	Harrah 3b	4	0	1	0
Bosetti cf	3	0	0	0	Charboneau lf	3	0	0	0
Ainge 3b	2	0	0	0	Kuiper 2b	3	0	0	0
Woods ph	1	0	0	0	Veryzer ss	3	0	0	0
Martinez c	2	0	0	0					
Whitt ph	1	0	0	0					
Totals	27	0	0	0	Totals	32	3	7	3

Toronto	000	000	000 — 0
Cleveland	200	000	01x — 3

E — Mayberry, Garcia, Griffin. LOB — Toronto 0, Cleveland 6. HR — Orta (2). SF — Thornton.

	IP	H	R	ER	BB	SO
Toronto						
Leal L2-4	8	7	3	1	0	5
Cleveland						
Barker W3-1	9	0	0	0	0	11

T — 2:09   A — 7,290.

STATISTICAL LEADERS

HOME RUNS	John Mayberry 17
RBIs	John Mayberry 43, Lloyd Moseby 43
BATTING AVERAGE	Damaso Garcia .252
STOLEN BASES	Damaso Garcia 13
WINS	Dave Stieb 11
ERA	Roy Lee Jackson 2.61
STRIKEOUTS	Dave Stieb 89
SAVES	Joey McLaughlin 10

HIGHS

- May 11 – Toronto obtains catcher Buck Martinez from Milwaukee for outfielder Gil Kubski. Martinez went on to become a key leader on the team as it emerged as a division power in the mid 1980s.

- After a disastrous 16–42 record prior to the strike, the Jays rebound with a respectable 21–27 record when play resumes.

- Despite his 11–10 record, Dave Stieb pitches superbly and appears headed for stardom.

LOWS

- May 15 – The Jays' weak bats are completely stifled when the Indians' Len Barker throws a perfect game at Cleveland Municipal Stadium. Barker was an average pitcher who won 74 games in eleven seasons spent with four teams.

- Between May 31 and June 11, the Jays lose a team record twelve straight games.

- August 17 – things are not looking up in the second half of the season as the Jays commit three errors in the fourth inning while losing 5–3 in Kansas City.

First Half Dozen To Suit Up for the Blue Jays and Expos

1. Ron Fairly   Montreal 1969–74, Toronto 1977

Fairly drove in 1,044 runs in a fine 21-year career and played over 1,000 games each in the outfield and infield. He also earned the distinction of playing with the Expos and Jays in both of their inaugural seasons and was the Jays' first-ever representative in the All-Star game.

2. Hector Torres   Montreal 1972, Toronto 1977

An accomplished fielder who could play three infield positions, Torres' main drawback was that he could not hit with consistency. He retired after the 1977 season with a career batting average of only .216 but went down in history as the first Toronto player to hit a grand slam. Since becoming a major league instructor with the Jays in 1979, Torres has coached at every level in the Jays system to the present.

3. Balor Moore   Montreal 1970–1974, Toronto 1978–1980

The veteran left-handed pitcher won a career-high nine games with the Expos in 1972. He played his last major league season with the Jays in 1980 after posting a career mark of 28–48 with a 4.52 ERA.

4. Tom Hutton   Toronto 1978, Montreal 1978–81

Hutton was a reserve outfielder and clubhouse leader during a solid 12-year career. He played 64 games for the Jays in 1978 before moving on to the Expos where he led the popular bench corps known as the "BUS Squad" which stood for "Broke Underrated Superstars."

5. Jim Mason   Toronto 1977, Montreal 1979

Mason was a back-up infielder for nine major league seasons beginning with the old Washington Senators in 1971. He was a solid fielder but hit under .200 in seven of his nine years.

6. Tony Solaita   Montreal 1979, Toronto 1979

A decent hitter and outfielder, Solaita split the 1979 season between Canada's two major league franchises. His finest effort came in 1975 when he hit 16 home runs for the Kansas City Royals.

Player Profile

Dave Stieb

One of the finest pitching careers in a Blue Jay uniform was put forth by right-hander Dave Stieb. Originally an outfielder, the Jays decided to switch Stieb to the pitcher's mound in 1978. This proved to be an astute manoeuvre as he went on to become the Jays' all-time winningest hurler. Remarkably, many of his wins came on a relatively weak team. Fortunately for Stieb he was still with the club when it won its first division title in 1985, and inaugural World Series seven years after that.

During Toronto's dismal season in 1979, Stieb turned in a respectable 8–8 mark as a starter. The next year he won twelve games and made his first of seven all-star game appearances. While the Jays and the league struggled through the strike-shortened 1981 and 1982 seasons, Stieb emerged as an elite starter. His slider was considered by many to be the best in the game while he also generated a great deal of movement on his fastball. Stieb went on to win at least fifteen games on six occasions, flirt with a no-hitter three times and eventually held the Cleveland Indians hitless in 1990. The cantankerous right-hander was also notorious for his intense scowl when things did not go his way out on the mound.

Along the way the combative right-hander was a part of four division winners and was a role player on Toronto's first World Series team in 1992. The next year he pitched briefly for the Chicago White Sox then made a surprise return to the Jays five years later as a long reliever and emergency starter. A week before his 41st birthday, Stieb made his first start in six years for Toronto when he was pressed into service during the second game of a double header versus the Chicago White Sox. Stieb retired for good in 1998 as the Jays' all-time leader with 175 wins and 1,658 strikeouts.

Quotes

"What the hell, we can't be any worse than we were before."
Bobby Mattick on the fresh start afforded each team in the second half of the strike-marred 1981 season.

"The Blue Jays are unnecessarily bad – so bad that they must be what they are as a result of choice, because nobody could be that bad by accident."

Bill James

1982

78–84 .481 6th-tie

The Season

For the first time the Blue Jays played competitive baseball through an entire season. The combination of young players coming of age and the managing savvy of Bobby Cox elevated Toronto's fortunes. Toronto came close to the elusive .500 mark record while finishing 17 games behind the powerful Milwaukee Brewers. Along the way they served notice that the club had the potential to be closer to the top the next season.

Several elements of a contender began to take shape over the course of the 1982 schedule. The starting rotation was of a high standard with Dave Stieb, Jim Clancy and Luis Leal combining for 45 wins. Stieb set a team record with five shutouts and Clancy became the first Toronto pitcher to flirt with a no-hitter. Rookie Jim Gott rode a blazing fastball to a 5–10 record in 30 appearances while Dale Murray, Roy Lee Jackson and Joey McLaughlin led the bullpen. Murray proved to be the best closer with 11 saves in 111 innings pitched but he was not as dominant as the other top short relievers in the American League.

A key transaction saw veteran John Mayberry traded to the Yankees for Dave Revering and Jeff Reynolds to make room for Willie Upshaw as the everyday first baseman. The youngster responded with 21 home runs and 75 RBIs while becoming the club's most consistent offensive producer. Upshaw's emergence salvaged the Jays on this deal since Revering was unproductive and lazy while Reynolds failed to reach the major leagues. Second baseman Damaso Garcia enjoyed a fine season with a .310 batting average, 58 stolen bases and 89 runs scored. Jesse Barfield broke through with 18 round trippers and 15 assists to give Toronto two-thirds of a solidified outfield. A well known proponent of platooning, Cox teamed Garth Iorg and Rance Mulliniks at third base while Ernie Whitt and Buck Martinez split the catching responsibilities.

Bobby Cox

STATISTICAL LEADERS

HOME RUNS	Willie Upshaw 21
RBIs	Willie Upshaw 75
BATTING AVERAGE	Damaso Garcia .310
STOLEN BASES	Damaso Garcia 58
WINS	Dave Stieb 17
ERA	Roy Lee Jackson 3.06
STRIKEOUTS	Dave Stieb 141
SAVES	Dale Murray 11

HIGHS

◆ September 28 – Jim Clancy carries a no-hitter into the ninth inning during a 3–0 win over the Minnesota Twins. Randy Bush plays the spoiler by singling with none out.

◆ Dave Stieb solidifies his place as a bonafide star with a 17–14 record, 3.25 ERA and a franchise record five shutouts.

◆ The Jays and Indians finish only 17 games back of the Brewers, the closest last place clubs have ever been to a division winner since divisional play began in 1969.

LOWS

◆ April 9 – the Jays lose their home opener for the first time as the eventual east division champion Milwaukee Brewers display their power in 15–4 romp. Starter Mark Bomback never recovers and suffers through a disappointing 1–5 season.

◆ The Jays fail to receive the same level of production from the designated hitter position as their rivals (.238, 8–56).

September 29, 1982
TWINS 0 at JAYS 3
First Game

Minnesota	ab	r	h	rbi	Toronto				
Mitchell cf	4	0	0	0	Garcia 2b	4	0	1	0
Castino 2b	3	0	0	0	Iorg 3b	4	1	1	1
Brunansky rf	3	0	0	0	Bonnell cf	3	0	0	0
Hrbek 1b	3	0	0	0	Barfield rf	3	1	1	1
Ward lf	3	0	0	0	Nordhgn dh	3	0	0	0
Gaetti 3b	3	0	0	0	Roberts lf	3	0	0	0
Bush dh	3	0	1	0	Upshaw 1b	3	1	2	1
Wshngtn ss	3	0	0	0	Martinez c	3	0	1	0
Smith c	2	0	0	0	Griffin ss	3	0	1	0
Johnson ph	0	0	0	0					
Totals	**27**	**0**	**1**	**0**	**Totals**	**29**	**3**	**7**	**3**

Minnesota	000	000	000 — 2
Toronto	000	200	10x — 3

DP — Minnesota 2, Toronto 1. LOB — Minnesota 1, Toronto 2. 2B — Griffin. HR — Iorg (1), Barfield (16), Upshaw (21). SB — Garcia (54).

	IP	H	R	ER	BB	SO
Minnesota						
Viola L4-9	8	7	3	3	0	4
Toronto						
Clancy W15-14	9	1	0	0	1	2
T — 1:33.						

Longest Surnames on a Blue Jays Uniform

Chuck Hartenstein 1977 11 Letters
Right-handed reliever Chuck Hartenstein hadn't pitched in the majors since 1970 when he returned to appear in 13 games for the Jays in 1977. His best years were spent with the Cubs and Pirates in the late 1960s.

Todd Stottlemyre 1988–1994 11 Letters
An occasionally brilliant and often intense competitor, Stottlemyre won 69 games for Toronto where he began in relief then earned a place in the starting rotation. He was a member of the 1992 and 1993 World Series teams before joining the Oakland A's in 1995.

Mark Lemongello 1979 10 Letters
Erratic on and off the field, Lemongello cost the Jays starting catcher Alan Ashby in a decidedly one-sided trade with Houston. His 1–9 record was less memorable than his notorious and violent tantrums.

Dave Friesleben 1979 10 Letters
A journeyman starter and reliever, Friesleben ended his six-year career in the majors with a one-year stint in the Jays' bullpen. His

best years came with the San Diego Padres in the mid-70s when he won 31 games in four seasons.

Joey McLaughlin 1980–84 10 Letters
Thought to have immense potential when he was acquired from Atlanta, McLaughlin was not the long-term answer to the Jays' need for a closer. Overall he saved 31 games for the club but lost several important leads, especially in the 1983 pennant race.

Joey McLaughlin

Mike Sharperson 1987 10 Letters

Originally thought to be the Jays' future second baseman, Sharperson played briefly with the club before he was traded to the Dodgers where he was a utility infielder for seven years.

John Candelaria 1990 10 Letters

A premier starting pitcher for most of his career, Candelaria was used briefly in relief by Toronto during the 1990 season. The "Candy Man" enjoyed his finest season in 1977 when he went 20–5 for the Pittsburgh Pirates.

Mark Dalesandro 1998–1999 10 Letters

Dalesandro spent two seasons with the Jays where he was a versatile role player used as a catcher, outfielder and third baseman.

Player Profile

Willie Upshaw

The first player ever chosen by Toronto in the Rule 5 Draft (see page 26) in 1977, Upshaw proved to be one of the longest serving members of the organization. A first baseman with an excellent glove and above average bat, he was the cousin of NFL stars Gene and Marvin Upshaw. He was a serious competitor whose leadership eventually became as important as his statistical contributions to the team.

The development of Upshaw in the minor leagues and as a reserve with the big club allowed the Jays to trade veteran John Mayberry early in the 1982 season. Upshaw relished the chance to start and enjoyed a fine 21 home run and 75 RBI season. In 1983 he led the Jays' offence with 27 home runs and 104 RBIs as the team challenged for the division title and played over .500 for the first time. In addition, Upshaw was the first Toronto player to reach the 100 RBI plateau. The next year he suffered a wrist injury that curtailed his power.

Upshaw continued to be a decent contact hitter and helped the Jays win their first division title in 1985. His home run against the Yankees on October 5, 1985 provided momentum in the pennant-clinching victory. Upshaw's numbers dropped in 1986 and 1987 and he was eventually replaced by Fred McGriff. He played his last season in 1988 with the Cleveland Indians and retired with over 500 career RBIs. He later served as the Jays' minor league hitting instructor in 1991 and 1992 before he was hired as the Texas Rangers' batting coach. After the Rangers overhauled their staff, Upshaw returned to the Jays as a minor league hitting coach.

Quotes

"I'd been knocked down and picked myself up instead of having other people pick me up."

> Mormon convert Jim Gott reflecting on how his improved lifestyle made him a stronger person.

"He had to learn to handle failure for the first time in his life, and he had to do it on centre stage. But Moseby never changed. He never stopped approaching the plate with a swagger, eager and confident. He never sulked. He never stopped playing and joking. He never gave up and the Blue Jays never gave up on him."

> Alison Gordon on Lloyd Moseby finally fulfilling his potential.

1983

89–73 .549 4th

The Season

In Bobby Cox's second year as manager, the team fulfilled much of the promise that was evident in 1982. The Blue Jays enjoyed their first winning season and became a legitimate threat in the competitive AL East. Consequently, their fans were treated to the exhilaration and heartbreak of a pennant race. They led the American League with a .277 team batting average and posted an impressive 48–33 record at home. During one glorious stretch the Jays occupied first place for 32 days but this young team wasn't ready just yet. In the end, the Jays finished nine games behind an Orioles team that went on to lose only two playoff games in winning their first World Series since 1970.

Coming off a respectable 78–84 campaign, Toronto entered 1983 with a talented young nucleus. The outfield was promising with Lloyd Moseby and Jesse Barfield on the verge of stardom and Barry Bonnell providing steady if unspectacular play. Veteran Dave Collins was acquired to light a fire under the youngsters and add depth. The infield was also strong with Willie Upshaw at first base, Damaso Garcia on second, former AL rookie-of-the year Alfredo Griffin at shortstop and Garth Iorg at third.

The pitching staff was a mix of excitement and uncertainty. Starters Dave Stieb, Jim Clancy and Luis Leal were coming off strong years and much was expected of hard-throwing Jim Gott. The bullpen was a concern as neither Roy Lee Jackson nor Joey McLaughin had proven to be consistent at the major league level although the former was more versatile since he could start as well as pitch long and short relief. Veteran Randy Moffit was brought in to add leadership and stability.

Over the course of the schedule, a major boost to the club's fortunes was the production of Cliff Johnson and Jorge Orta from the designated hitter position, a long-standing sore spot with the club. Johnson was picked up from Oakland in exchange for original Blue Jay Alvis Woods while Orta was acquired from the Mets for young pitcher Steve Senteney. The duo combined for 34 home runs and 113 runs batted in while helping the team lead the AL with a .277 batting average. Upshaw and Barfield each belted 27 home runs and Moseby drove home 81 runners. Upshaw's 104 RBIs made him the first player in franchise history to drive in at least 100 runs. The Jays also picked up two cast-offs from other teams who would later play a huge role in the improved fortunes of the club. They claimed pitcher Doyle Alexander after he was released by the Yankees in June and drafted outfielder George Bell from the Phillies prior to the season.

As it turned out, the bullpen lacked a sure-fire closer and failed to hold the lead in several important late season games. One bright spot was team Rookie-of-the-Year Jim Acker who posted a 5–1 record in 38 appearances. The team's lack of big game experience showed when they wilted during key sets against the Orioles and Tigers. Notice was served, however, that the club was going to be a major factor in the division for a number of years.

STATISTICAL LEADERS

HOME RUNS	Willie Upshaw, Jesse Barfield 27
RBIs	Willie Upshaw 104
BATTING AVERAGE	Barry Bonnell .318
STOLEN BASES	Damaso Garcia, Dave Collins 31
WINS	Dave Stieb 17
ERA	Dave Stieb 3.04
STRIKEOUTS	Dave Stieb 187
SAVES	Randy Moffit 10

HIGHS

◆ Team records its first winning season and contends for the pennant.

◆ Team leads the American League in batting average and slugging percentage.

◆ Dave Stieb is selected to start the All-Star Game at Comiskey Park and gains the win as the American League conquers its National League counterparts for the first time since 1971.

LOWS

◆ Tippy Martinez picks several Blue Jays off first base in the tenth inning of a crucial game during the heat of the pennant race.

◆ The "bullpen by committee" fails during the stretch drive – particularly damaging is McLaughlin's penchant for giving up the long ball.

Barry Bonnell

Grouches and Hot-Heads

1. Mark Lemongello

An intense and hot-tempered pitcher, Lemongello often threw inanimate objects in the club house and occasionally sent balls in the direction of manager Roy Hartsfield after being pulled from a game. He was also seen punching himself in the jaw, gnawing on his shoulder and behaving irrationally towards fans.

2. Damaso Garcia

Blessed with speed, hitting ability and a fine glove, second baseman Garcia often appeared sullen and withdrawn. His behavior kept him from being a fan favorite and his personal frustration boiled over when he burned his uniform in 1986. A few years later he underwent life saving surgery for a brain tumor.

3. George Bell

A monster at the plate, Bell was also a handful for the media and his managers. Seemingly content at one moment, he would often turn surly and defensive the next. The pinnacle of his dissatisfaction came during spring training in 1988 when he refused to play when informed that he was slotted for DH duty in the upcoming season.

4. Dave Stieb

A brilliant and competitive right-hander who threw the first no-hitter in Blue Jays history, Stieb rarely appeared satisfied with his performance. He could be moody and it was always a battle when the time came to check on him at the mound or pull him from a game.

5. Doyle Alexander

A tricky pitcher, Alexander turned in a gem when the Jays clinched their first division title in 1985. Unfortunately, he resented anything but country music being played in the clubhouse and disliked Toronto to the point that he felt obligated to complain about the airport before leaving town for good. He returned to the AL in 1987 with the Tigers and helped his new team stun the Jays to win the division during the last week of the schedule.

Cliff Johnson

6. Cliff Johnson

Johnson was a tough out for most pitchers and often delivered clutch base hits throughout his career. He was also a grouch who often barked at the media and constantly scowled at the music and sound effects played over the public address system between pitches.

7. Dave Revering

Revering had the tools to be a good player but during a television interview with Howard Cosell he was quite open about his lack of desire to play hard and his disdain for the Jays' organization. Following one plate appearance, when he was stunned by a pitch that shattered his bat and rolled towards the infield, he waived his hand defiantly and didn't even bother to run to first base in the event that an error might have taken place.

8. Barry Bonnell

Bonnell was a solid outfielder with above average hitting ability who stuck to his beliefs as a player. One of these convictions was his opposition to female reporters in the dressing room – a situation he handled by barricading himself around his locker.

9. Jack Morris

The Jays knew what they were getting when they signed this crafty but cantankerous veteran pitcher. Morris set a team record with 21 wins in 1992 and was generally snarly and sarcastic with reporters. Among his treatise was that females did not belong in the clubhouse.

10. Kelly Gruber

Gruber was a fine third baseman with a big bat who once hit for the cycle at Exhibition Stadium. Towards the end of his tenure with the Jays he became over-sensitive concerning the media and fans' booing which caused his stay in Toronto to end on a sour note.

Player Profile

Lloyd Moseby

One of the first stars nurtured in the Blue Jays farm system, Moseby was a complete player. He hit for power and average, stole bases, and was an above average fielder and thrower from his centre field position. The Portland, Arkansas, native was a consistent performer who was well liked in the clubhouse and by the fans.

Moseby's potential was obvious as early as his one-year stint with Medicine Hat of the Pioneer League in 1978. His ascension through the organization was rapid; he didn't even play a full year of Triple A at Syracuse before he was recalled to Toronto in 1980. Moseby began his major league career in style by hitting two doubles and a home run in his first two games versus the Yankees. He finished with 46 RBIs in 389 at bats and continued to evolve as a player through the 1982 season.

In tandem with the rise of the Jays to competitive status, Moseby broke out in 1983 with 18 home runs, 81 RBIs and 27 stolen bases. The following year he drove in 92 runs and led the AL with 15 triples. By 1985, Moseby teamed with Jesse Barfield and George Bell to give Toronto one of the top outfields in baseball. This gifted trio was an integral part of the franchise's first AL East crown in 1985.

The likeable veteran registered a personal best 26 home runs and 96 RBIs during the heartbreaking 1987 season when the club coughed up a sure division title to Detroit during the last week of play. One of the quickest players in the AL, "Shaker" led the Jays in stolen bases five straight seasons between 1985 and 1989. Moseby's numbers eventually slipped and he joined the dreaded Tigers in 1990. He left the majors following the next season with 169 career home runs and a permanent place in hearts of a generation of Blue Jays supporters. Moseby played with the Yomiuri Giants of the

Japanese league in 1992 and 1993 and later coached in the Jays' minor league system in 1997 and 1998, and served as the team's first base coach in 1999.

Quotes

"They're a lot different than they used to be. In spring training, I tried tucking a fastball in on Jesse Barfield to move him off the plate and all he did was stand there, lift his arm and scowl."

Boston pitcher Dennis Eckersley on the change he observed in the Blue Jays during the 1983 season.

Although he ended up having a decent year, Dave Collins began 1983 slowly and barely hit his weight which caused him to quip, "[I don't] mind hitting .220 during day games because people seeing it on the scoreboard might think it was the time."

Alison Gordon, *Foul Balls*

Considering the impact Doyle Alexander had on the Jays during his brief tenure with the club, the following comments were amusing: "Now that the Blue Jays have signed Doyle Alexander, let me hedge on my pre-season pick of Toronto finishing second in the AL East. I take back all those nice things I said about Pat Gillick, the Jays' GM. How can the Birdbuilder louse up such a fine pitching staff by signing an underachiever like Alexander the Ingrate."

New York Post baseball writer Dick Young.

July 7, 1983
NL 3 at AL 13

National	ab	r	h	rbi	American				
Sax 2b	3	1	1	1	Carew 1b	3	2	2	1
Hubbard 2b	1	0	1	0	Murray 1b	2	0	0	0
Raines lf	3	0	0	0	Yount ss	2	1	0	1
Madlock 3b	1	0	0	0	Ripken ss	0	0	0	0
Dawson cf	3	0	0	0	Lynn cf	3	1	1	4
Drvecky p	0	0	0	0	Wilson cf	1	0	1	1
Perez p	0	0	0	0	Rice lf	4	1	2	1
Orosco p	0	0	0	0	Oglivie rf	1	0	0	0
Bench ph	1	0	0	0	Young p	0	0	0	0
L Smith p	0	0	0	0	Quisnbrry p	0	0	0	0
Oliver 1b	2	1	1	0	Brett 3b	4	2	2	1
Evans 1b	1	0	0	0	Simmons c	2	0	0	0
Murphy rf	3	0	1	1	Parrish c	2	0	0	0
Guerrero 3b	1	0	0	0	Cooper ph	1	1	1	0
Schmidt 3b	3	0	0	0	Boone c	0	0	0	0
Benedict c	1	0	1	0	Winfield rf	3	2	3	1
Carter c	2	0	0	0	Kittle lf	2	1	1	0
Durham rf	2	0	0	0	Trillo 2b	3	1	1	0
OSmith ss	2	1	1	0	Whitaker 2b	1	1	1	2
McGee cf	2	0	1	0	Stieb p	0	0	0	0
Soto p	1	0	0	0	DeCinces ph	1	0	0	0
Hammakr p	0	0	0	0	Honeycutt p	0	0	0	0
Dawley p	0	0	0	0	Ward ph	1	0	0	0
Thon ss	3	0	1	0	Stanley p	0	0	0	0
					Henderson lf	1	0	0	1
					Ystrzmsk ph	1	0	0	0
Totals	**35**	**3**	**8**	**2**	**Totals**	**38**	**13**	**15**	**13**

National	100	110	000 — 3	
American	117	000	22x — 13	

GW-RBI — Yount. E — Stieb, Carew, Schmidt, Sax, Guerrero. DP — American 2. LOB — National 6, American 9. 2B — Winfield, Oliver, Wilson, Brett. 3B — Brett, Whitaker. HR — Rice, Lynn. SB — Sax, Raines. S — Stieb. SF — Brett, Yount, Whitaker.

	IP	H	R	ER	BB	SO
National						
Soto (L)	2	2	2	0	2	2
Hammaker	2/3	6	7	7	1	0
Dawley	1 1/3	1	0	0	0	1
Dravecky	2	1	0	0	0	2
Perez	2/3	3	2	2	1	1
Orosco	1/3	0	0	0	0	1
L. Smith	1	2	2	1	0	1
American						
Stieb (W)	3	0	1	0	1	4
Honeycutt	2	5	2	2	0	0
Stanley	2	2	0	0	0	0
Young	1	0	0	0	0	1
Quisenbrry	1	1	0	0	0	1

PB — Benedict. T — 3 :05. A — 43,801.

1984

89–73 .549 2nd

The Season

The Jays matched their win total from 1983 and in many ways were an improved team. They enjoyed a brilliant 28–14 start but suffered from being in the same division as a Detroit Tigers squad that began the season 35–5 and never looked back. On June 5, Willie Aikens, Ernie Whitt and Alfredo Griffin hit home runs to lead the Jays to an 8–4 win in Tiger Stadium and brought the club within $4^1/_2$ games of first place. Detroit refused to falter, however, and the Jays' wins seemed to be matched by the Tigers on most nights.

During the second half of the season the Jays lost a lot of close games and did not fare well in head-to-head competition with the Tigers as their rivals held an 8–5 edge in the season series. Particularly damaging was the Motowners' 4–2 record at Exhibition Stadium. Towards the end of the season the club lost some of its drive when Detroit was too far ahead. Had the Tigers not set such a blazing pace, the Jays would likely have topped the 90-win mark for the first time.

The starting staff was the strength of the team's pitching. The foursome of Doyle Alexander, Dave Stieb, Luis Leal and Jim Clancy combined for 59 wins. Jim Acker, rookie Jimmy Key, Roy Lee Jackson and Dennis Lamp were solid but the club lacked a dominant stopper in the mould of Detroit's Willie Hernandez or Kansas City's Dan Quisenberry. Jackson and Key were effective at times but one of the key stats for Toronto from the 1984 season was that 34 losses were traceable to the bullpen.

Speedy outfielder Dave Collins was the team's most consistent offensive threat and was named the team's player of the year for his efforts. George Bell broke through with 26 home runs while veteran DH Cliff Johnson, Willie Upshaw and Lloyd Moseby had productive seasons. The third base platoon of Garth Iorg and Rance Mulliniks was solid while Ernie Whitt and Buck Martinez complemented each other behind the plate. Jesse Barfield and Tony Fernandez improved but were a year away from becoming full-time impact players. The Jays were a fine team in 1984 but were still a step away from being a contender – regardless of the Tigers dream season.

STATISTICAL LEADERS

HOME RUNS	George Bell 26
RBIs	Lloyd Moseby 92
BATTING AVERAGE	Rance Mulliniks .324
STOLEN BASES	Dave Collins 60
WINS	Doyle Alexander 17
ERA	Dave Stieb 2.83
STRIKEOUTS	Dave Stieb 198
SAVES	Roy Lee Jackson, Jimmy Key 10

HIGHS

◆ June 2 – Jays win their team record 19th consecutive one-run game.

◆ July 20, 1984 – Jays send a team record 16 batters to the plate and score 11 runs in the ninth inning of a 12–7 win over the Seattle Mariners.

◆ August 5 – Cliff Johnson sets a new major league record by hitting his 19th career pinch hit home run. During a 15-year career spent with five teams, Heathcliff hit 196 round trippers and drove in 699 runs.

◆ Between August 24 and 27 Rance Mulliniks sets a team record (later tied by Paul Molitor) with eight consecutive hits.

LOWS

◆ Willie Aikens is unable to improve the Jays' production from the DH spot and hits just .205 before heading back to the minors. A feared power hitter with California and Kansas City between 1978 and 1983, Aikens' substance abuse problems kept him from playing a long career.

◆ The Jays struggle to a 10–16 record against the Yankees and the front-running Tigers.

Ten Highest Single Season Batting Averages by a Blue Jay
(minimum 200 at bats)

John Olerud

1. John Olerud .363 1993

The soft-spoken owner of one of the game's sweetest swings, Olerud flirted with the elusive .400 mark as late as August. He ultimately settled for his first batting title and second World Series ring.

2. Carlos Delgado .344 2000

The heart of the Jays' batting order in the cleanup spot, Delgado chased the triple crown for much of the year despite the loss of number 3 hitter Raul Mondesi at mid-season. He also set new team records with 137 RBIs and 57 doubles.

3. Paul Molitor .341 1994

Molitor was a menace to opposing pitchers in a disappointing year for Toronto. Before the season was shut down in August, he already had 155 hits and was one of the few Jays to play consistently well.

4. Paul Molitor .332 1993

Located in the enviable position between Roberto Alomar and Joe Carter in the Jays' batting order, Molitor hit for average and power in 1993. His bat, hustle and clubhouse leadership were integral factors behind Toronto's second consecutive World Series title.

5. Robert Perez .327 1996

Perez barely qualified with 202 at bats but no one can take away from the consistency and poise he demonstrated at the plate in his first full season. He was one of the few bright lights in the Jays' disappointing fourth-place finish in 1996.

6. Roberto Alomar .326 1993

One of the most complete players of his era, Alomar was a crucial offensive weapon and defensive stalwart in the Jays' repeat World Series season. The second-base star hit at least .300 in four of his five seasons in Toronto.

7. Rance Mulliniks .324 1984

A reliable hitter and fielder, Mulliniks helped the Jays stay reasonably close to the nearly unbeatable Tigers for most of the 1984 season. The likeable third baseman topped the .300 batting mark three times with Toronto.

8. Tony Fernandez .323 1987

Fernandez enjoyed his finest season to date when the Jays led the AL East for most of the 1987 schedule. In addition to his high batting average, the gifted shortstop drove in 67 runs and stole 32 bases.

9. Tony Fernandez .321 1998

Fernandez's third stint in Toronto showed that he had plenty of pop in his bat at the age of 36. He drove in a career high 72 runs and still managed to swipe 13 bases while finishing among the top ten in the AL batting race.

10. Barry Bonnell .318 1983

Bonnell was a decent outfielder with an above average bat who played for the Jays while they were waiting for the young outfield of Bell-Moseby-Barfield to develop. He recorded 187 RBIs while platooning in the Toronto outfield for four seasons.

Player Profile

Damaso Garcia

Second baseman Damaso Garcia was a top-notch talent in the field and at the plate. For years he formed an effective double-play combination with Alfredo Griffin, and then Tony Fernandez. Garcia also managed to hit at least .280 in five of his seven seasons in Toronto and took part in two all-star games.

The native of Moca, Dominican Republic, was acquired in a multi-player trade with the New York Yankees on November 1, 1979. At spring training he won the job as starting second baseman. As a rookie he hit .278 and stole 13 bases while soldifying the Jays' middle infield.

Injuries and the strike-shortened schedule limited Damo's playing time in 1981. But by 1982 he was recognized as one of the best young second basemen in the American League. He hit a career best .310 and stole 54 bases and was a key factor in the improved fortunes of the club under Bobby Cox. Damo was a model of consistency by going hitless in back-to-back games only once all season. Garcia was selected to play in consecutive all-star games in 1984 and 1985. When he helped Toronto win its first division title in 1985, Garcia recorded personal highs of 8 home runs and 65 RBIs.

An emotional competitor, Garcia suffered through a frustrating year in 1986 as the team stumbled and he managed only 424 at bats. He resented new manager Jimy Williams' plan to shift him from leadoff to ninth in the batting order. Garcia's frustration boiled over in May when he burned his uniform after a game in which he made two costly errors. He spent a year away from the majors before returning for two final seasons with the Braves and Expos. Garcia retired with a lifetime batting average of .283 and later won a successful battle against a life-threatening brain tumor. He settled in the Dominican Republic and served as the players association director of the country's top baseball league.

Quotes

"Baseball is not a game that needs a new statistic. It is already awash in enough of them to take on Stats Canada and the *Globe*'s *Report on Business* simultaneously."

Trent Frayne

"But at least the Jays could come close this year, go through the pressure cooker of the pennant race, give their fans a fun season and come back next year as a qualified contender."

Al Strachan of *The Globe and Mail* writing in June 1983.
Had the Tigers not stunned the majors with their
35–5 start, he might have been more accurate.

Rance Mulliniks

July 21, 1984
JAYS 12 at MARINERS 7

Toronto	ab	r	h	rbi	Seattle				
Garcia 2b	5	1	1	1	Prconte 2b	5	0	2	1
Collins lf	3	1	1	0	Owen ss	5	2	3	0
Moseby cf	5	2	2	2	Davis 1b	3	2	1	4
Upshaw 1b	5	1	2	1	Phelps dh	1	0	0	0
Leach 1b	0	1	0	0	Milbourn dh	2	0	0	0
Aikens dh	4	0	1	1	Cowens rf	4	0	2	2
Griffin dh	1	1	1	1	Putnam lf	3	0	0	0
Mulliniks 3b	3	0	1	1	Bonnell lf	1	0	0	0
Johnson ph	1	0	1	0	Presley 3b	4	0	0	0
lorg 3b	1	2	0	0	Kearney c	4	1	2	0
Whitt c	3	0	1	0	Bradley cf	4	2	2	0
Bell ph	1	1	1	0					
Martinez c	0	0	0	0					
Barfield rf	5	1	3	2					
Fernandz ss	4	1	2	2					
Totals	41	12	17	11	**Totals**	36	7	12	7

Toronto	000	000	10(11)	— 12
Seattle	001	001	014	— 7

GW-RBI — Fernandez (2). E — Presley. DP — Toronto 1, Seattle 1. LOB — Toronto 6, Seattle 6. 2B — Barfield, Collins, Upshaw. 3B — Perconte, Moseby. HR — Davis (19). SB — Bradley (13), Garcia (29).

	IP	H	R	ER	BB	SO
Toronto						
Clancy	6 2/3	5	2	2	3	5
Key	1	2	1	1	1	0
Acker W3-5	1/3	1	0	0	0	0
Jackson	1	4	4	4	0	0
Seattle						
Beattie	7 1/3	6	1	1	2	2
Stanton	1	2	2	2	0	1
Mirabella L1-4	0	4	4	4	0	0
Nunez	0	1	2	2	1	0
Geisel	2/3	4	3	3	1	1

Mirabella pitched to 4 batters in 9th; Nunez pitched to 2 batters in 9th. WP — Clancy. Balk — Key. PB — Whitt. T — 3:34. A — 8,246.

1985

99–62 .615 1st
Lost American League Championship

The Season

The Jays earned their first post-season trip in only their ninth year of existence. It was the culmination of careful drafting and the development of players at all levels of the minor league system. There were a few trades and the odd free agent signing but Toronto's rise in the American League was chiefly a result of building from within. For pitcher Jim Clancy, infielder Garth Iorg and catcher Ernie Whitt, the division title was particularly sweet since they had been with the club since its debut in 1977.

Veteran right-hander Doyle Alexander led the way with 17 wins and fittingly pitched the division-clinching game against the Yankees in October. The switch from the bullpen to the starting rotation turned Jimmy Key into a potential star as he won 14 games with an impressive 3.00 ERA. Stieb and Clancy were also solid as was journeyman Tom Filer who won seven games as an injury fill-in during the latter stages of the season. Jim Acker and veterans Gary Lavelle and Dennis Lamp provided solid middle relief. Bill Caudill was acquired from Oakland in a pre-season deal to serve as the closer but he was inconsistent and the club's pennant hopes were kept alive by rookie Tom Henke's stellar work after being called up in July.

The Bell-Barfield-Moseby combination led the way on offence while Willie Upshaw, Ernie Whitt and Cliff Johnson took turns providing key hits. The re-acquisition of Johnson was a key move as veterans Jeff Burroughs and Len Matuszek failed to deliver from the

DH spot. Johnson's patience at the plate was crucial during the latter stages of the season as he delivered many runners with an array of solid and bloop singles as well as a few timely home runs. Veteran Al Oliver was acquired in July from the L.A. Dodgers in exchange for the disappointing Matuszek. Iorg and Mulliniks combined for 94 RBIs at third base while Garcia and Fernandez excelled in the middle infield.

The lineup was replete with talent and enthusiasm but there was a distinct lack of big game experience. This was exposed in the American League championship series against the Kansas City Royals when the Jays blew a 3–1 series lead, dropping the last three games to miss out on the World Series. Toronto missed a golden opportunity to wrap up the series in five games but wasted a fine pitching effort by Jimmy Key and Jim Acker and lost game five 2–0. Still, 1985 was a special year for the team and its fans as they had a chance to feel the exhilaration and heartbreak of elevated expectations.

STATISTICAL LEADERS

HOME RUNS	George Bell 28
RBIs	George Bell 95
BATTING AVERAGE	Garth Iorg .313
STOLEN BASES	Lloyd Moseby 37
WINS	Doyle Alexander 17
ERA	Tom Henke 2.03
STRIKEOUTS	Dave Stieb 167
SAVES	Bill Caudill 14

HIGHS

◆ May 1 – Jimmy Key becomes the first left-handed starter to win a game since Paul Mirabella on October 4, 1980.

◆ June 6 – Buck Martinez hits the game-winning home run in the bottom of the 12th inning to give the Jays a 1–0 win in the opening game of a crucial series versus the Tigers. Unfortunately, he suffered a season-ending injury a few weeks later in Seattle.

◆ October 5 – Ron Hassey of the Yankees flies out to George Bell giving the Jays their first-ever division title.

◆ October 6 – Veteran Phil Niekro wins his 300th game as the Yankees beat the Jays to close out the season.

◆ October 8 – The Jays whip Kansas City 6–1 in the first major league playoff game ever held in Canada.

LOWS

◆ October 4 – Butch Wynegar hits a home run off Tom Henke with two out in the ninth inning to postpone their title celebrations by one day.

◆ October 16 – The Kansas City Royals complete their comeback from a 3–1 deficit by winning 6–2 in the deciding game of the AL championship series.

Fastest Trips to the Post-Season by an Expansion Team

1. Arizona Diamondbacks 1999 Year 2

Following a 65–97 inaugural season, the Diamondbacks spent a great deal of money upgrading the roster with starting pitcher Randy Johnson, outfielder Steve Finley and second baseman Tony Womack. They won the NL West but lost to the wild card New York Mets in the divisional series.

2. Colorado Rockies 1995 Year 3

The Rockies adapted to the thin air of their home field by assembling solid hitters such as Dante Bichette, Vinny Castilla and free agent Larry Walker. Oddly enough, the Rockies' only win in their 3–1 loss to Atlanta in the divisional series came on the road.

Devon White

3. Florida Marlins 1997 Year 5

The Marlins spent freely in 1996 and 1997 then hit the jackpot in their fifth year by winning the World Series. Key acquisitions such as Kevin Brown, Al Leiter, Devon White, Gary Sheffield and Moises Alou helped the team defeat San Francisco, Atlanta and then Cleveland.

4. New York Mets 1969 Year 8

Beginning with their disastrous 120–loss season in 1962, the Mets were cellar dwellers in each of their first four years. In 1969 they stunned the favoured Baltimore Orioles to win the World Series with starting pitchers Tom Seaver and Jerry Koosman leading the way.

5. Kansas City Royals 1976 Year 8

The Royals won 85 games in their third year and remained competitive while waiting for the Oakland A's dynasty to end. In their first playoff series they lost a five-game AL championship series to the New York Yankees.

6. Toronto Blue Jays 1985 Year 9

The Jays won 99 games to edge out the Yankees and earn a match up with the Kansas City Royals. After taking a 3–1 lead, their inexperience showed and they lost out in seven games.

October 6, 1985

YANKEES 1 at JAYS 5

New York	ab	r	h	rbi	Toronto				
RHndsn cf	4	0	0	0	Garcia 2b	5	0	1	1
Griffey lf	4	1	1	0	Moseby cf	2	1	1	1
Mattingly 1b	4	0	1	0	Upshaw 1b	4	1	2	1
Winfield rf	4	0	1	1	Oliver dh	2	1	1	0
Hassey c	4	0	0	0	C Jhnsn dh	2	0	1	0
Baylor dh	3	0	1	0	Mulinks 3b	1	0	0	0
Pagliarulo 3b	3	0	0	0	G Iorg 3b	3	0	2	0
Rndlph 2b	3	0	1	0	G Bell lf	3	0	0	1
Meacham ss	2	0	0	0	Whitt c	4	1	1	1
Pasqua ph	1	0	0	0	Barfield rf	4	0	1	0
K Smith ss	0	0	0	0	Fernndz ss	4	1	2	0
Totals	**32**	**1**	**5**	**1**	**Totals**	**34**	**5**	**12**	**5**

New York	000	100	000 — 1
Toronto	013	100	00x — 5

GW-RBI — Whitt (8). E — Hassey. DP — New York 1. LOB — New York 4, Toronto 8. 2B — Barfield, Oliver, Griffey, Fernandez. HR — Whitt (19), Moseby (18), Upshaw (15). SB — Moseby (37), Winfield (19). SF — G Bell.

	IP	H	R	ER	BB	SO
New York						
Cowley L12-6	2¹/₃	4	3	3	1	0
Shirley	0	2	1	1	0	0
Bordi	1	2	1	1	1	0
Rasmussn	¹/₃	0	0	0	0	1
N. Allen	4¹/₃	4	0	0	0	0
Toronto						
Alexander W12-10	9	3	1	1	0	0

Shirley pitched to 2 batters in 3rd. WP — N. Allen. T — 2:38. A — 44,688.

Player Profile

Tony Fernandez

One of the slickest fielders in the game and possessing a sharp eye at the plate, Fernandez enjoyed three successful stints in a Toronto uniform. Able to play second and third base as well as his natural position of shortstop, Fernandez became the Jays' all-time leader in career hits on July 4, 1998.

One of the best players from the "baseball factory" of San Pedro de Macoris, Dominican Republic, Fernandez's progress through the Toronto system allowed the club to part with Alfredo Griffin in 1984. During Tony's first season as a starter in 1985, he hit .289 and helped the team win its first division title. He became one of the most respected shortstops in the game and appeared in three all-star games in the late 1980s helping the club win its second division crown in 1989. His injury late in the 1987 season probably cost Toronto the division title.

In December 1990 he was sent to San Diego with Fred McGriff in the trade that brought Joe Carter and Roberto Alomar to Toronto. Tony played two seasons with the Padres and the first part of the 1993 schedule with the New York Mets before the Jays reacquired him to add depth to their attempt to repeat as World Series winners. Fernandez hit .306 that year and the Jays won their second straight World Championship. He next played with Cincinnati, and the New York Yankees, and then helped Cleveland reach the World Series in 1997. The Jays signed him as a free agent in 1998 and he spent two years contributing to the club's resurgence before moving to the Japanese league.

Quotes

"A fight is a fight; but we're all ballplayers, we're all basically in the same mould, and we just don't do anything like that. Buckner's action was ugly; it was really uncharacteristic of a baseball fight."

Buck Martinez commenting on Boston's Bill Buckner kicking
Jays' coach John Sullivan in the face during the infamous
brawl started when George Bell karate-kicked
Bruce Kison after being hit by a pitch.

"He progressed along the basepaths at a terrific clip. A terrific clip for Heathcliff. Unfortunately what is a terrific clip for Johnson could easily be mistaken for the speed at which eras plod across the pages of history. Johnson slid into third with all the stately grace of an ocean liner docking. He would have been out if the Royals' fielder had sent the throw by Canada Post."

Joey Slinger of the *Toronto Star* summed up Cliff Johnson's
failed attempt to stretch a double into a triple
in game 2 of the AL championship series.

"As much as any pitching problems, it will be the Jays' inability to cash in on scoring opportunities that will haunt them this winter. In their final three futile jousts they left the basepaths littered with stranded bodies – crying and pleading for deliverance."

Garth Woolsey, *Toronto Star* October 17, 1985

Dave Winfield

1986

86–76 .531 4th

The Season

The Jays' tenth season was full of outstanding individual performances but the team failed to repeat as division winners following Bobby Cox's departure to Atlanta and subsequent replacement by Jimy Williams. When starters Dave Stieb and Jimmy Key struggled at the beginning, this was too much for the talented club to overcome.

The key problem was a lack of consistency from its starting pitchers. Stieb was a very mortal 7–12, Doyle Alexander was 5–4 before a trade sent him to Atlanta and Jim Clancy battled to a 14–14 mark. Although Jimmy Key finished 14–11 after a brilliant second half, he unfortunately struggled along with the rest of the team during its poor start. The average work by the starters wasted the stellar work of long reliever Mark Eichhorn and closer Tom Henke. A versatile performance was turned in by lefty John Cerutti who won 9 games as a starter and reliever.

Toronto's batting order and defence stacked up with the best in the majors. The outfield of Barfield, Bell and Moseby combined for 92 home runs and 302 RBIs while Tony Fernandez, Cliff Johnson, Ernie Whitt and Rance Mulliniks each hit double figures in home runs. Fernandez's range at shortstop and Barfield's speed and powerful arm earned them the first two Gold Gloves in franchise history. The Iorg-Mulliniks platoon at third and the Martinez-Whitt duo behind the plate continued to function smoothly but Willie Upshaw and Damaso Garcia had sub-par years. When the last out was recorded, there was a sense that spring training couldn't arrive fast enough.

STATISTICAL LEADERS

HOME RUNS	Jessie Barfield 40
RBIs	Jessie Barfield, George Bell 108
BATTING AVERAGE	Tony Fernandez .310
STOLEN BASES	Lloyd Moseby 32
WINS	Jim Clancy, Mark Eichhorn, Jimmy Key 14
ERA	Mark Eichhorn 1.72
STRIKEOUTS	Mark Eichhorn 166
SAVES	Tom Henke 27

HIGHS

◆ June 27 – second baseman Damaso Garcia ties a major league record with four doubles versus the Yankees.

◆ July 10 – Garcia becomes the first player to register 1,000 hits as a Blue Jay.

◆ July 28 – Jim Clancy becomes the first Blue Jay pitcher to win 100 games.

◆ September 22 – Tony Fernandez becomes the first Blue Jay player to register 200 hits in a season.

LOWS

◆ The team drops from first to fourth in Jimy Williams' first year as manager.

◆ Dave Stieb suffers through an uncharacteristic 7–12 season with a 4.74 ERA.

First Ten Blue Jays Pitchers to Win at Least 10 Games

Jerry Garvin

Lefty Jerry Garvin began the season 5–0 before running into inconsistency and lack of run support. He finished the year 10–18 but later developed into a solid relief pitcher for the club.

Dave Lemanczyk

Not much was said about Lemanczyk at the start of the 1977 season even though the former Detroit Tiger ended up being the club's top winner with a 13–16 mark. His effort was recognized by his selection as the team's pitcher-of-the-year.

Jim Clancy

Clancy enjoyed a solid 10–12 record in 1978 but this was just a sign of things to come. He went on to reach double figures in wins seven more times and left the franchise as the second winningest pitcher of all time with 128. His success was anticipated by the Jays who made him their third choice in the expansion draft when they plucked him from the Texas Rangers' organization.

Dave Stieb

Stieb was the first superstar pitcher to wear a Jays' uniform. He won twelve games in 1980 then later won at least 15 games six times and threw the first no-hitter in franchise history in 1990.

Luis Leal

A solid right-hander, Leal won twelve games in 1982 before recording consecutive 13 win seasons in 1983 and 1984. He retired after the 1985 season with a career record of 51–58. The popular right-hander was known for his control and swivel delivery based on the well-known Luis Tiant.

Doyle Alexander

Luis Leal

A wily right-hander who was successful in both leagues, Alexander recorded a fine 17–6 record in 1984 when he was named the team's top pitcher. He matched that total in 1985 and was on the mound when the Jays clinched their first division title with a 5–1 win over the Yankees. Alexander won 194 games in a fine 19-year career spent with nine different teams.

Jimmy Key

Lefty Jimmy Key started as a short reliever but his career improved dramatically when he was shifted to the starting rotation. In 1985 he won 14 games in his first year as a starter and helped Toronto win the AL East.

Dennis Lamp

Originally brought to the Jays as a closer, sinker ball specialist Dennis Lamp was best suited to long relief. In 1985 he posted an impressive 11–0 record and formed an ideal set-up team with veteran Gary Lavelle.

Mark Eichhorn

Sidearm reliever Mark Eichhorn took the American League by storm in 1986 with ten saves and a 14–6 record. He hit double figures in wins again from the bullpen in 1987 and retired in 1996 with career totals of 48 wins and 32 saves.

John Cerutti

Left-hander Cerutti was a versatile starter and reliever for six seasons with the Jays. He recorded his first of two 11–win seasons in
1987 and was a member of two division championships. Cerutti
played one season in Detroit before retiring in 1981 with 49 career
wins.

Jeff Musselman

Musselman enjoyed an excllent rookie season out of the Jays
bullpen in 1987 when he won 12 games and made 68 appearances.
He started 15 games for the club the next season then spent two
years with the New York Mets before leaving the majors.

Player Profile

Jessie Barfield

Barfield was an impressive combination of
power and defence while playing right field
for the Jays from 1981 to the early part of the
1989 season. He was blessed with a fluid
swing at the plate and one of the strongest outfield arms in baseball. During the 1980s Barfield
combined with George Bell and Lloyd Moseby to
become the best young outfield in the majors.

The native of Joliet, Illinois, hit .232 as a part-time player in
1981 then drove in 58 runs in only 394 at bats in 1982. His production at the plate and his stolen base total would have been
higher had he not suffered a knee injury. The Jays had such high
hopes for Barfield that they agreed to part with speedy outfielder
Dave Collins in the trade that brought Bill Caudill east. He hit at
least 25 home runs on four occasions including 27 when the Jays

won their first division title in 1985 and an AL-best 40 in 1986. In both 1985 and 1986 he led all American League rightfielders in assists, putouts and double plays while recording fielding percentages of .989 and .992.

Barfield hit 179 career home runs in Toronto but was sent to the Yankees in exchange for left-handed pitcher Al Leiter when the team re-adjusted during its poor start in 1989. He continued to hit the long ball consistently in the Bronx before retiring in 1992 with career totals of 241 home runs and 716 RBIs.

Quotes

". . . a good bullpen makes a manager a lot smarter."

Bobby Cox

"The Blue Jays haven't been discovered yet as being as formidable a club as they are."

Cleveland President Peter Bavasi on why a strong club like Toronto was such a poor draw on the road.

Jim Clancy

JAYS 14 at YANKEES 7

Toronto	ab	r	h	rbi	New York				
Ferandz ss	6	2	2	2	Rhndsn cf	6	1	2	4
Garcia 2b	6	3	4	1	Winfield rf	5	0	0	0
Moseby cf	6	2	3	3	Mtngly 1b	5	1	3	1
Bell lf	5	2	2	1	Easler dh	5	0	2	0
Barfield rf	4	1	2	5	Griffey lf	5	1	2	1
Iorg 3b	2	1	1	2	Hassey c	2	0	0	0
Mulliniks 3b	3	0	1	0	Wynegar c	3	1	1	0
Bmartnz c	2	0	0	0	Pagliarulo 3b	5	1	4	0
Whitt c	3	1	1	0	Rndlph 2b	4	1	2	0
Gruber dh	1	0	0	0	Berra ss	2	1	2	1
Leach dh	4	2	2	0	Pasqua ph	0	0	0	0
					Fischlin ss	1	0	0	0
Totals	47	14	19	14	Totals	43	7	10	7

Toronto	204	000	332 — 14
New York	121	210	000 — 7

GW-RBI — Barfield (8). E — Pagliarulo 2, Alexander, Iorg. DP — Toronto 3. LOB — Toronto 7, New York 12. 2B — Garcia 4, Bell, Upshaw. 3B — Moseby. HR — Mattingly (13), Iorg (2), Griffey (9), RHenderson (14), Barfield (19), Fernandez (4). SB — Pagliarulo (2). S — Berra. SF — Barfield.

	IP	H	R	ER	BB	SO
Toronto						
Alexander	3	8	6	6	1	1
Cerutti	1 1/3	3	1	0	0	1
Acker W2-3	2 1/3	3	0	0	0	1
Henke S9	2 1/3	4	0	0	1	1
New York						
Guidry	2 2/3	7	6	6	0	3
Drabek	2 2/3	1	0	0	0	1
Holland	1 1/3	1	1	0	0	1
Fisher L4-4	1/3	2	2	0	0	0
Shirley	2	8	5	5	0	2

Alexander pitched to 2 batters in 4th. T — 3:38. A — 30,815.

1987

96–66 .593 2nd

The Season

Prior to the last week of the regular season the Blue Jays were putting forth an effort that ranked with their future World Series years. They were the most balanced team in the majors: deep in pitching, hitting, speed and defence. Toronto even had the benefit of the 1985 playoff experience to aid their preparation for the 1987 pennant race with the Detroit Tigers. On paper the Blue Jays were clearly superior but their rivals outplayed them down the stretch including a tight three-game series at Tiger stadium to close the season.

Six Toronto pitchers won at least 10 games and the staff posted an ERA of 3.74 to lead the American League. The starting rotation of Stieb, Key and Clancy was bolstered by the late-season acquisition of veteran Mike Flanagan. John Cerutti and Jeff Musselman perfomed well as both starters and relievers while Eichhorn and Henke were a dream combination in the late innings.

The Jays boasted a powerful line-up that clubbed 215 home runs, the sixth highest in league history. After hitting .308 with 47 home runs and 134 RBIs, outfielder George Bell was chosen the most valuable player in the American League. Barfield, Moseby, Whitt, Upshaw, Mulliniks, Cecil Fielder, Kelly Gruber and Fred McGriff all hit at least ten home runs. The club's 845 runs would be topped only by the 1993 championship team.

Although the end result was disappointing, the 1987 pennant race was one of the most exciting periods for Canadian fans. This was especially so in southwestern Ontario where many friends and families were split between the Tigers and Jays. The two clubs battled through seven one-run games late in the season ranging from the emotional match-up in Toronto where Tony Fernandez was injured and lost for the season to the final weekend showdown in Motown. Toronto entered with a one-game lead but were swept to finish two games back. Manny Lee was the unlikely source of a three-run homer in the opener but the Tigers came from behind to win with little-used Scott Lusader hitting a neat round tripper. In the second game Detroit veteran Jack Morris pitched ten stellar innings while lefty Frank Tanana tossed a gem the next day to beat Jimmy Key 2–1 and stun the Jays who had looked like a World Series calibre club two weeks earlier.

STATISTICAL LEADERS

HOME RUNS	George Bell 47
RBIs	George Bell 134
BATTING AVERAGE	Tony Fernandez .322
STOLEN BASES	Lloyd Moseby 39
WINS	Jimmy Key 17
ERA	Tom Henke 2.49
STRIKEOUTS	Jim Clancy 180
SAVES	Tom Henke 34

HIGHS

◆ June 24 – shortstop Tony Fernandez plays in his team record 403rd consecutive game.

◆ July 14 – George Bell starts for the American League in the All-Star Game after becoming the first Toronto player selected by the fans.

◆ September 14 – The Jays set an American League record by hitting ten home runs during an 18–3 thrashing of the Baltimore Orioles. The onslaught was led by Ernie Whitt who became the second Toronto player after Otto Velez to hit three home runs in a single game.

◆ December 8 – George Bell is named the American League's most valuable player and the player of the year in the major leagues by The Sporting News.

LOWS

◆ September 24 – In a controversial attempt to break up a double play, Detroit's Bill Madlock runs into Tony Fernandez who lands on the frame surrounding the dirt at second base, breaking his elbow.

◆ October 4 – Frank Tanana outpitches Jimmy Key 2–1 to clinch the AL East pennant for the Tigers.

First Ten Blue Jays Catchers

1. Phil Roof

On October 22, 1976, Roof was the first player acquired by the Blue Jays when his rights were obtained from the Chicago White Sox. During the 1977 season he played his last three big league games but failed to record a hit.

2. Rick Cerone

Although he was the second-string catcher in 1977, Cerone started in the club's inaugural game against the White Sox. After Alan Ashby was traded to Houston, Cerone drove in 61 runs in 1980 before he was sent to the New York Yankees.

3. Alan Ashby

The Jays' first number-one catcher, Ashby struggled at the plate in 1977 but improved to hit .261 the next season. In one of the Jays' worst trades, he was sent to Houston for erratic pitcher Mark Lemongello; Ashby then enjoyed eleven productive seasons with the Astros.

4. Ernie Whitt

Whitt was not a favorite of Jays' manager Roy Hartsfield and thus did not get a legitimate chance to make the club until Bobby Mattick took over in 1980. Ernie eventually became one of the most popular Toronto players as he hit at least 10 home runs for eight straight seasons and was one of the three original Jays on hand when the club won its first division title in 1985.

5. Brian Milner

Milner played his only two big league games for the Jays in 1978. His claim to fame was being the youngest to ever suit up for the Jays at 18 years, seven months and six days on June 23, 1978. Three days later he had three hits in Toronto's 24–10 romp over the Orioles.

6. Bob Davis

Playing parts of five seasons with the Padres before backing up Cerone in 1979 and Whitt in 1980, Davis retired in 1981 after eight seasons as a part-time player.

7. Pat Kelly

Kelly was called up from the minors in 1980 and took part in three games where he managed two hits. This was his only taste of the big leagues.

8. Mike Macha

Macha played a handful of games for the Atlanta Braves in 1979 before joining Toronto the next season. He played briefly at third base and catcher for the Jays before returning permanently to the minors.

9. Ken Macha

No relation to Mike, Ken Macha joined Toronto in 1981 after two decent seasons as a back-up in Montreal where he hit .278 and .290. He struggled with his adjustment to the American League before retiring in 1981 after playing six seasons in the majors.

10. Buck Martinez

From 1981 to 1986, the right-handed hitting Martinez was the perfect platoon partner with the left-handed hitting Ernie Whitt. A solid team leader, Martinez provided stellar defensive work, a few hits and helped Toronto win its first division title in 1985. Fifteen years later, he became the club's eighth manager after a successful career as a television analyst.

Player Profile

George Bell

A multi-talented star with a volatile personality, George Bell made a lasting impression on the Toronto sporting scene in the 1980s. His quickness and power at the plate were unquestionable but at times his emotions got the better of him on the field and in the clubhouse. His immense talent outweighed his unpredictable behaviour and he combined with Jessie Barfield and Lloyd Moseby to form one of the top outfields in baseball.

One of Pat Gillick's shrewdest moves was plucking Bell from the Philadelphia Phillies' organization in 1980 via the Rule 5 Draft. He was initially a spot player in 1981 and 1983 before seizing a starting position and launching 26 home runs in 1984. Bell contributed 28 round trippers in 1985 and caught the last out when the team clinched its first playoff spot with a 5–1 win over the Yankees.

His greatest individual performance came in 1987 when he hit 47 home runs and drove in 134 runners on the way to being named the American League's Most Valuable Player. During one series at Comiskey Park in August he hit two home runs over the left field roof and became one of a handful of sluggers to reach the centre-field bleachers when he victimized Tom Seaver. The only sore spot was that Bell, like the rest of the team, played poorly during the last week of the season.

Prior to the 1988 season his deteriorating relationship with manager Jimy Williams exploded when he refused to bat in a spring training game in protest over the team's plans to make him the regular DH instead of left fielder. Despite the fireworks, Bell recorded RBI totals of 97 and 104 in 1988 and 1989. His inspired play under new manager Cito Gaston helped the club win its second division title in 1989.

After a sub-par 1990 season, Bell was not retained by the club as it retooled for the decade ahead. He played a year with the Chicago Cubs before joining the crosstown White Sox for his last two big league seasons. In 1992 he drove in 112 runs and retired in 1993 with 265 home runs and 1,002 RBIs. He spent the early part of his retirement with his wife and six children. He attended the Jays' 1997 minor league spring training as a guest instructor and was brought on board for the rest of the season. Since 1998 he has served as the club's minor league roving hitting instructor.

Quotes

"Sorry for what? What − you just get fired or something?"
Phil Niekro responding to a writer who had offered condolences after hearing of the veteran pitcher's release by the Jays.

When asked if he would be telephoning Tony Fernandez to apologize for knocking him out for the remainder of the season, Bill Madlock of the Tigers snapped, "Why should I? I'm not the welcome wagon."

Jimmy Key

```
                    September 15, 1987
                 ORIOLES 3 at JAYS 18
Baltimore    ab  r  h  rbi  Toronto
Stanick dh    5  0  0   0   Liriano 2b     4  3  3  1
BRipken 2b    3  1  1   0   Moseby cf      4  1  1  2
Sheets rf     4  1  2   0   Ducey cf       2  1  1  3
Murray 1b     4  0  3   0   Fernndz ss     4  0  1  1
CRipken ss    4  0  2   2   Lee ss         2  1  1  0
RWgtn ss      0  0  0   0   G Bell lf      4  2  2  2
Knight 3b     4  0  0   0   Thortn lf      1  1  1  0
Gonzales 3b   0  0  0   0   Whitt c        5  3  3  5
Kennedy c     3  0  0   0   Barfield rf    5  1  4  0
CNichols c    1  0  1   0   Mulliniks 3b   3  2  2  3
M Young lf    4  0  0   0   Gruber 3b      2  0  0  0
Hart cf       4  1  2   1   McGriff dh     4  2  1  1
                           Upshaw 1b      4  1  1  0
Totals       36  3 11   3   Totals        44 18 21 18
Baltimore            001    001   010 — 3
Toronto              052    111   71x — 18
```

GW-RBI — Whitt (7). DP — Baltimore 1, Toronto 1. LOB — Baltimore 7, Toronto 6. 2B — Murray, C.Ripken, Liriano, Barfield. HR — Whitt 3 (17), Mulliniks 2 (10), Moseby (23), G Bell 2 (45), Ducey (1), McGriff (19), Hart (4).

	IP	H	R	ER	BB	SO
Baltimore						
Dixon L7-10	1²/₃	5	5	5	1	2
E. Bell	1¹/₃	2	2	2	0	1
MGriffin	2	3	2	2	2	0
Kinnunen	1²/₃	6	6	6	1	0
Arnold	1²/₃	5	3	3	0	0
OConnor	²/₃	0	0	0	0	1
Toronto						
Clancy W13-10	7	7	2	2	1	6
Eichhorn	1	2	1	1	0	1
Henke	1	2	0	0	0	0

WP — Clancy. T— 3:18. A — 27,446.

1988

87–75 .537 3rd-Tie

The Season

Much was expected of the Blue Jays in 1988 following the stunning loss to the Tigers in the previous year's pennant race. It was widely believed that Toronto was the most talented team in baseball and that this would be the year they put everything together. However the team suffered through a slow start and didn't attain consistency until after the All-Star break. Toronto recorded the most wins of any AL East team in the second half of the schedule but lost out in a tight race that saw the Red Sox win their second division championship in three years.

As usual there was plenty to like about the Jays on paper. Dave Stieb won 16 games and Mike Flanagan proved to be more than a rental from the 1987 pennant drive by gaining 13 victories of his own. The staff led the American League with 17 shutouts while Tom Henke and Duane Ward combined for 40 saves. Concern over Jimmy Key's arm troubles was alleviated by his solid 12–5 record during the latter half of the season.

First baseman Fred McGriff built on the flashes of brilliance he demonstrated in 1987 by clubbing an AL-high 34 home runs. He also hit .282 and led Toronto with 100 runs scored. Bell, Gruber and Whitt also enjoyed fine years at the plate but Jessie Barfield slumped to 18 home runs and a .244 batting average. Manny Lee and Tony Fernandez were an effective double play combo and newcomer Pat Borders did a good job platooning with the veteran Whitt behind the plate. The team led the AL with 158 home runs and a .419 slugging percentage and the pitching staff's ERA was comparable to 1987. The main fault of the club was that its 22–7 resurgence in September and October came too late.

Mike Flanagan

STATISTICAL LEADERS

HOME RUNS	Fred McGriff 34
RBIs	George Bell 97
BATTING AVERAGE	Rance Mulliniks .300
STOLEN BASES	Lloyd Moseby 31
WINS	Dave Stieb 16
ERA	Tom Henke 2.91
STRIKEOUTS	Dave Stieb 147
SAVES	Tom Henke 25

HIGHS

◆ April 4 – George Bell sets an opening day record by hitting three home runs in the Jays' 5–3 win over the Kansas City Royals. All three shots came at the expense of starter Bret Saberhagen. The temperamental outfielder followed up his MVP season with a solid, if unspectacular, 24 home run and 97 RBI performance.

◆ April 11 – In their home opener, the Jays pound the Yankees 17–9.

◆ June 4 – the Jays complete their first ever four-game sweep of the Red Sox at Fenway Park.

◆ September 24 & 30 – In two of the greatest consecutive starts in history, Dave Stieb carries no-hitters for 8 2/3 innings first against the Cleveland Indians and then the Baltimore Orioles. Julio Franco spoiled the first one while Jim Traber's single past Fred McGriff ended the second no-hit attempt.

◆ George Bell is the only individual named the American League player of the week twice.

LOWS

◆ March 17 – during a Grapefruit League game against the Red Sox, George Bell refuses to bat as the team's designated hitter.

◆ The team drops nine games off the previous year's pace in a very winnable division.

◆ Star outfielder George Bell's strained relationship with manager Jimy Williams distracts the team at various times during the season.

Unsung Heroes

1. Tony Castillo

Castillo began his career with the Jays but was most effective during his second stint with the club from 1993 to 1996 when his ERA was consistently among the lowest on the team. His solid work out of the bullpen versus left-handed batters was an important part of the club's World Series repeat in 1993.

2. John Cerutti

Left-hander John Cerutti toiled in the shadow of the Jays' more celebrated pitchers but was a tireless workhorse as a starter and reliever for six seasons. He won 46 games for Toronto and logged many innings in the thankless job of long relief.

3. Garth Iorg

The right-handed hitting half of a successful third base platoon with Rance Mulliniks, Iorg was a hard worker for nine seasons. He played all 931 career games in Toronto and was one of three original Jays on hand when the team took its first division title in 1985.

Roy Lee Jackson

4. Roy Lee Jackson

Although he did not end the Jays' search for a dominant closer, over four seasons Jackson saved 30 games and was a solid situational reliever utilizing an intimidating fastball. He was a stable influence in the clubhouse where he helped support such youngsters as Jesse Barfield when they were struggling and also chipped in by singing the national anthem on occasion.

5. Rance Mulliniks

Mulliniks was a solid hitter, outstanding fielder and positive influence in the Jays' clubhouse from 1982 to 1992. Three times he hit at least .300 and between 1984 and 1986 he led all American League third basemen in fielding percentage.

6. Dan Plesac

An upbeat influence in the clubhouse, Plesac made over 100 appearances for the Jays between 1997 and 1999 when he was called upon in a number of different situations. He proved to be a valuable left-hander out of the bullpen and averaged more than one strikeout per inning. Plesac returned to the Jays as a free agent in 2001 to add depth to the pitching staff.

Player Profile

Fred McGriff

Owner of a smooth and powerful swing, first baseman Fred McGriff was one of the shrewdest acquisitions by general manager Pat Gillick. In December, 1982, the Jays sent veteran reliever Dale Murray to the Yankees for speedy outfielder Dave Collins, pitcher Mike Morgan and a young McGriff. Collins provided offensive spark and leadership for two years while McGriff developed in the minors before hitting 20 home runs as a rookie in 1987.

The sweet swing of McGriff launched 105 home runs between 1988 and 1990. The popular first basemen led the American League with 36 round trippers in 1989 when he helped the Jays win their second division title. That year he was also credited with the first home run ever hit out of Skydome.

In December 1990 he was packaged with Tony Fernandez in the deal with the San Diego Padres that landed Joe Carter and Roberto Alomar. McGriff led the National League with 35 home runs in 1992 and later joined the Atlanta Braves where he won his first World Series ring in 1992. The native of Tampa, Florida, joined the hometown Devil Rays in 1998 where he provided leadership and power to the young franchise.

Quotes

"We'll see who lasts longer in this organization, me or Jimy."

George Bell venting during the controversy with manager Jimy Williams over him assuming the duties of DH in the 1988 season.

"I got too many things on my mind to be happy right now."

George Bell after hitting three home runs on opening day from the DH spot.

"It was a really good curve – down and in. It almost hit him. When it came off the bat, I thought I had it [the no-hitter]. A second later, I knew it was gonna fall in."

Dave Stieb reflecting on the 9th-inning hit by Baltimore's Jim Traber that spoiled his second no-hit bid in less than a week.

April 5, 1988								
JAYS 5 at ROYALS 3								
Toronto	ab	r	h	rbi	**Kansas C.**			
Liriano 2b	4	0	0	0	WWilsn cf	5	1	2 0
Moseby lf	4	1	0	0	Seitzer 3b	3	1	1 1
Fernndz ss	4	0	0	0	Brett dh	5	1	2 2
GBell dh	4	3	3	4	Trtabll rf	4	0	2 0
Mulinks 3b	4	1	1	0	FWhite 2b	4	0	1 0
Gruber 3b	0	0	0	0	Balboni 1b	3	0	0 0
Whitt c	4	0	1	0	Madisn 1b	1	0	0 0
Barfield rf	3	0	1	1	BJacksn lf	4	0	1 0
McGriff 1b	4	0	2	0	Macfarln c	4	0	2 0
Campsn cf	4	0	1	0	Stilwll ss	4	0	0 0
Totals	35	5	9	5	**Totals**	37	3	11 3

Toronto   010   300   010 — 5
Kansas City   200   000   100 — 3

GW-RBI — G.Bell (1). E — Balboni. LOB — Toronto 5, Kansas City 9. 2B — Macfarlane 2, Tartabull 2, Mulliniks, B.Jackson, Campusano, McGriff. 3B — Wilson. HR — Brett (1), G.Bell 3 (3). SB — Seitzer (1). S — Liriano. SF — Barfield, Seitzer.

	IP	H	R	ER	BB	SO
Toronto						
Key W1-0	6	8	2	2	1	4
Wells	1/3	2	1	1	0	0
Eichhorn	2/3	1	0	0	0	0
Henke S1	2	0	0	0	0	1
Kansas City						
Sabrhgn L0-1	8	7	5	3	0	7
Quisnberry	1	2	0	0	0	0

T — 2:58. A — 40,648.

1989

89–73 .549 1st
Lost American League Championship

The Season

The Blue Jays turned one of the most dismal starts in franchise history into their second division title. The catalyst of the improvement was new manager Cito Gaston who guided the club to a 77–49 record after being promoted from batting coach. The Jays also bid adieu to Exhibition Stadium and played their first game at Sky-Dome on June 5. Although the hiring of Gaston was a positive step for the team, it wasn't until August that the wins came in abundance and the team became a legitimate threat to win the division.

Dave Stieb was the undisputed leader of the starting rotation but he was ably followed by lefties Jimmy Key, Mike Flanagan and John Cerutti. Mauro Gozzo caused a stir by coming out of nowhere to go 4–1 in mid-season and Todd Stottlemyre began to assert himself as a regular in the line-up. The excellent tandem of Ward and Henke led the bullpen while David Wells excelled in long relief.

There was no shortage of power in the Toronto batting order with Fred McGriff's 36 home runs and George Bell's 104 RBIs leading the way. Spark was provided by rookie Junior Felix and the mid-season addition of Mookie Wilson and Lee Mazzilli. The Jays tore through August. The surprise was that the showdown came versus the Baltimore Orioles, a team that went a record 0–21 to start the 1988 season on the way to 107 losses.

After clinching their second trip to the playoffs, the Jays ran into an Oakland team that, for once, played the same way in the post-season as the previous 162 games. Toronto fought gamely but lost in five games to the A's who went on to crush San Francisco in the World Series which was marred by the Bay area earthquake. For Toronto, 1989 ushered in the Cito Gaston era that would lead to greater success. It also brought fans a division title that had been so frustratingly elusive over the previous three seasons.

STATISTICAL LEADERS

HOME RUNS	Fred McGriff 36
RBIs	George Bell 104
BATTING AVERAGE	Mookie Wilson .298
STOLEN BASES	Lloyd Moseby 24
WINS	Dave Stieb 17
ERA	Jim Acker 1.59
STRIKEOUTS	Duane Ward 122
SAVES	Tom Henke 20

HIGHS

◆ April 16 – Kelly Gruber becomes the first Blue Jays' player to hit for the cycle when he victimizes the Kansas City Royals.

◆ May 28 – George Bell's home run in the bottom of the 11th inning gives the Jays a 7–5 win over the Chicago White Sox in the last game played at Exhibition Stadium.

◆ June 3 – The Jays overcome a 10–0 deficit to defeat the Red Sox 13–11. Ernie Whitt's grand slam and Junior Felix's aggressive play at the plate and on the basepaths unhinged the Red Sox.

◆ August 4 – Dave Stieb throws a perfect game for $8^2/3$ innings before the Yankees' Roberto Kelly plays the spoiler with a single.

◆ September 30 – The Jays beat the Orioles 4–3 to win their second division title.

LOWS

◆ May 15 – In the first mid-season managerial change in franchise history, the 12–24 Jays replace Jimy Williams with Cito Gaston in an attempt to salvage their season.

◆ June 5 – The Blue Jays drop their SkyDome opener 5–3 to the Milwaukee Brewers.

◆ The Oakland A's prove too powerful for the Jays and win the AL championship series in five games.

Exhibition Stadium and SkyDome

First Games:

Exhibition Stadium:
April 7 , 1977
Toronto Blue Jays 9   Chicago White Sox 5
 * last game May 28, 1989
Toronto Blue Jays 7   Chicago White Sox 5

SkyDome:
Milwaukee Brewers 5   Toronto Blue Jays 3
June 5, 1989

First Winning pitcher:
Exhibition Stadium:
Jerry Johnson
SkyDome:
Don August

First Home Run:
Exhibition Stadium:
Richie Zisk
SkyDome:
Fred McGriff

First Playoff Game:
Exhibition Stadium
October 8, 1985
Toronto Blue Jays 6   Kansas City Royals 1
SkyDome:
October 6, 1989
Toronto Blue Jays 7   Oakland A's 3

Manager Profile

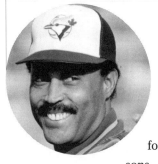

Cito Gaston

Known as a players' manager who was always loyal to his veterans, Cito Gaston was the breath of fresh air the Jays desperately needed after they stumbled out of the gate in 1989. A former major league outfielder during eleven seasons, he was brought in as the Jays' first full-time batting instructor in 1982. Gaston's impact was immediate as the team batting average improved from .226 to .262 in one year. He remained a key figure in the team's offensive production under Bobby Cox and Jimy Williams.

After a dreadful 12–24 start in 1989, the organization looked to Gaston as an interim solution to get the Jays to live up to their immense potential. The team relaxed and looked sharper under Cito and the club responded by hiring him as the full-time manager after 15 days of being the temporary answer. Cito's managerial performance was one of the top stories in baseball in 1989. The club settled down and slowly got back in the division race before dominating the league in August to secure its second division title. The Jays finished a disappointing second in 1990, then lost the AL championship series to Minnesota in 1991.

A fine blend of youthful and veteran talent was handled superbly by Gaston in 1992 and 1993 when Toronto won consecutive World Series. The team struggled between 1994 and 1997 as a result of free agent losses and injuries. Gaston was relieved of his position late in 1997 with the club sporting a 72–85 record. He later returned in 1999 as the club's batting instructor and was a major reason why the club's offence was among the best in the American League in 2000.

Quotes

"We've changed our thinking to go with somebody from the outside, somebody with a different relationship with the players."

> Pat Gillick commenting on the search for a full-time manager to take over from interim skipper Cito Gaston.

"I was talking with Jimy this morning. I wish he could've been here. It was great to be part of this."

> Cito Gaston after the Jays' first game at SkyDome.

Todd Stottlemyre

June 4, 1989									
BLUE JAYS 10 at RED SOX 2									
Toronto	ab	r	h	rbi	Boston				
Felix rf	5	0	3	4	Boggs 3b	4	0	2	1
Fernndz ss	5	0	1	0	Barrett 2b	4	0	0	0
Infante ss	0	0	0	0	Heep 1b	2	0	1	0
Gruber 3b	4	0	0	0	Esasky 1b	1	0	0	0
G.Bell lf	4	1	0	0	Greenwl lf	4	0	1	0
Ducey lf	0	0	0	0	Evans rf	3	1	1	0
McGriff 1b	4	3	2	1	Burks cf	4	1	2	0
Moseby cf	5	3	3	1	Horn dh	2	0	0	0
Whitt c	4	1	0	0	Quintan dh	2	0	1	0
Mlinks dh	2	1	1	1	Gedman c	4	0	1	1
Liriano 2b	4	1	3	3	Romero ss	4	0	0	0
Totals	37	10	13	10		34	2	9	2

Toronto		010	401	031 —10
Boston		020	000	000 — 2

E — Burks, Evans. DP — Toronto 1, Boston 1. LOB — Toronto 6, Boston 7. 2B — Mulliniks, Burks, Greenwell. HR — McGriff (12), Moseby (6). SB — Moseby (10), Liriano (7).

	IP	H	R	ER	BB	SO
Toronto						
Stieb W4-3	5	7	2	2	2	2
Wells	3	2	0	0	0	2
Henke	1	0	0	0	0	2
Boston						
Boddickr L3-5	5²/3	9	6	5	3	3
Lamp	1¹/3	2	3	3	3	1
Price	1	1	0	0	0	0
LSmith	1	1	1	1	0	1

Lamp pitched to 4 batters in the 8th.
T — 3:05. A — 33,942.

1990

86–76 .531 2nd

The Season

Despite a mediocre season by Toronto standards, the team remained in the thick of the pennant race until the last week of play. When they fell short against Baltimore and division winner Boston in key late season match ups, their fate was sealed. A number of new faces contributed to the team's winning record and established themselves as regulars as the franchise built towards the success that was to follow in the early 1990s.

Pitching was a problem in 1990 as Dave Stieb and youngster David Wells were the only starters to enjoy a solid year. Both Todd Stottlemyre and Jimmy Key won 13 games but struggled with ERAs over 4.00. Toronto was unable to get much use out of veterans Mike Flanagan, John Candelaria and Bud Black. The Henke and Ward duo pitched well in the bullpen but had fewer leads passed on to them to protect.

Third baseman Kelly Gruber joined Fred McGriff as a bonafide star but Bell and Felix were not consistent. Pleasant surprises came in the form of rookies Glenallen Hill and John Olerud but there was a lack of offensive cohesion in the day-to-day batting order. Tony Fernandez put forth a solid effort at shortstop but was hampered by a lack of consistency at second base from Manny Lee and Nelson Liriano. Mookie Wilson was probably the most consistent hitter among the Jays outfield brigade but overall the production was down from this section of the roster.

STATISTICAL LEADERS

HOME RUNS	Fred McGriff 35
RBIs	Kelly Gruber 118
BATTING AVERAGE	Fred McGriff .300
STOLEN BASES	Tony Fernandez 26
WINS	Dave Stieb 18
ERA	Tom Henke 2.17
STRIKEOUTS	Dave Stieb 125
SAVES	Tom Henke 32

Mookie Wilson

September 3, 1990
JAYS 3 at INDIANS 0

Toronto	ab	r	h	rbi	Cleveland				
MWilsn dh	4	0	0	0	Cole cf	2	0	0	0
TFrndz ss	4	0	2	0	Browne 2b	4	0	0	0
Gruber 3b	3	0	0	0	DJames lf	3	0	0	0
McGriff 1b	4	2	2	2	Phelps dh	2	0	0	0
Borders c	4	0	1	0	Jacoby 1b	3	0	0	0
GHill lf	4	0	1	0	Baerga ss	2	0	0	0
Willims cf	4	1	1	0	Snyder rf	3	0	0	0
Lee 2b	4	0	1	1	Brokns 3b	2	0	0	0
Felix rf	3	0	0	0	CJams ph	1	0	0	0
					Skinner c	2	0	0	0
					Maldonado ph	1	0	0	0
Totals	**34**	**3**	**8**	**3**	**Totals**	**25**	**0**	**0**	**0**

Toronto	000	110	001 — 3
Cleveland	000	000	000 — 0

E — D.James. LOB — Toronto 5, Cleveland 2. 2B — Williams, Lee. HR — McGriff 2 (31).

	IP	H	R	ER	BB	SO
Toronto						
Stieb W17-5	9	0	0	0	4	9
Cleveland						
Black L10-9	7	5	2	2	1	5
Orosco	1	2	1	1	0	1
Olin	1	1	0	0	0	0

Orosco pitched to 1 batter in the 9th. WP — Black. T — 2:27. A — 23,640.

HIGHS

◆ May 9 – The Jays defeat the Chicago White Sox 4–3 for the 1000th regular season win in franchise history.

◆ June 8–17 – The Jays complete their most successful road trip ever by winning nine out of ten against Milwaukee, Minnesota and New York.

◆ September 3 – Dave Stieb fires the first no-hitter in Blue Jays' history by shutting out the Indians 3–0 at Cleveland Stadium. The final out was recorded when Jerry Browne flew out to Junior Felix.

◆ September 19 – The Jays break the L.A. Dodgers' single season home attendance record and finish the year over 3.8 million.

◆ The Jays commit only 86 errors, the second lowest total in American League history at that time.

LOWS

◆ June 29 The Jays are stymied by Oakland's Dave Stewart who throws a no-hitter at them in a 5–0 victory.

◆ The Jays' pinch hitters are a dismal .216 with no home runs and 14 RBIs.

Flashes in the Pan

Doug Ault

Ault was the hero of the Jays' first win (over the White Sox) when he hit two home runs. He went on to record eleven home runs and 64 RBIs in 1977 but a hitch in his swing caused his production to slip to the point that he wasn't even invited to spring training in 1979.

Victor Cruz

Cruz burst on to the scene with a 7–3 record and nine saves in 1978 before he was traded to Cleveland in the deal that brought Alfredo Griffin to Toronto. Cruz was an average pitcher for two years with the Indians then played sparingly for Pittsburgh and Texas before retiring.

Steve Davis

Davis gave the Jays 28 strong innings in 1985 and became the first 20-game winner in the organization when his minor league totals were included. He only pitched in fifteen big league games after that season and became a career minor leaguer.

Junior Felix

Junior Felix

A talented and popular addition to the Jays when they overcame a slow start to win the division in 1989, Felix hit 15 home runs the next year before his lackadaisical attitude wore thin. He played with three more teams but left the majors in 1994 after a six-year career that began with so much promise.

Tom Filer

Not in Toronto's plans in 1985, Filer nevertheless pitched well – going 7–0 when the Jays ran into injury problems. His solid performance helped keep the team in first place but he did not sustain this momentum and retired in 1992 with only 22 career victories.

Mauro Gozzo

"Goose" Gozzo pitched well in nine appearances for the Jays in 1989 but he could not sustain his success. After his 4–1 season with the Jays he pitched sparingly in Cleveland then went 3–5 for the Yankees in 1994 before leaving the majors.

Steve Staggs

Staggs showed some potential at second base for the Jays in their inaugural season when he hit .259 and scored 37 runs. He was released and played in 47 games for Oakland in 1978 before leaving the majors.

Player Profile

Kelly Gruber

A fiery competitor blessed with a strong arm and a natural instinct at the plate, Gruber played nine years in Toronto and was a member of the franchise's first World Series triumph in 1992. He played all but 18 of his 939 regular season games with the Jays and was an integral part of the club's success in the late 1980s and early 90s.

The native of Houston, Texas, got a taste of the majors in 1984 and 1985, then played in 87 games in 1986. His first full season was the heartbreak of 1987 when the club slumped late in the season and the Tigers won the division. Gruber's best years were from 1988 to 1991 when he averaged 21 home runs and 84 RBIs and was selected to play in two All-Star games.

On April 16, 1989, Gruber became the first Toronto player to hit for the cycle when he victimized three Kansas City Royals' pitchers. Gruber was a mainstay on the Jays as they won their first division title since 1985. In 1990 he enjoyed his finest season with 31 home runs and 118 RBIs although the club failed to repeat as playoff participants. In 1991 he hit 20 home runs and helped the club win its third division title.

He was a member of the Jays' 1992 World Series team but struggled at the plate after hurting his neck while swinging as a pitch. An emotional player, Gruber let the fans' booing get to him and he occasionally vented his frustration through the media. He was traded to California prior to the 1993 season where he was injured most of the year and eventually retired with 443 career RBIs. In 1985 he underwent spinal fusion surgery as a result of his original neck injury.

Quotes

"I was calm all night. I threw a one-hitter against Seattle two years ago. The leadoff hitter got a base hit, then I retired the next 27 batters."

Dave Stewart after throwing a no-hitter for Oakland
versus the Jays at SkyDome.

"I had to give up caring about them. Even today, it wasn't going to be the end of the world if I didn't get it. If I don't, the worse that happens is well, nothing."

Dave Stieb after throwing the first no-hitter by a Toronto pitcher
— after several close calls in the past.

1991

91–71 .562 1st
Lost AL Championship Series

The Season

The Jays shook up part of their roster in preparation for the 1991 season. Toronto traded starting infielders Fred McGriff and Tony Fernandez to the San Diego Padres for Joe Carter and Roberto Alomar. The club also signed veteran centre fielder Devon White as a free agent. In the short run, a division title was obtained but, more significantly, the seeds of World Series success were sown.

After years of leading the starting rotation Dave Stieb was limited to nine games. Fortunately, Jimmy Key, David Wells and Todd Stottlemyre each won at least 15 games and Juan Guzman burst on to the scene with a 10–3 record. Midway through the season young outfielders Mark Whiten and Glenallen Hill were sent to the Indians for veteran knuckleballer Tom Candiotti. In the bullpen Jim Acker, Bob MacDonald and Mike Timlin pitched well before handing off to Duane Ward and Tom Henke who combined for 55 saves.

Carter was a well-known power hitter and he came through as expected with 33 home runs. White played superbly in centre field and hit for power with 17 round trippers of his own. Right field was more problematic with only veteran Candy Maldonado playing well in spurts. Alomar was everything the Jays hoped for at second base and more. His combination of speed, power and defence were of a superstar quality. The Jays struggled to replace McGriff at first base as rookie John Olerud hit 17 home runs but lacked experience. Although a decent fielder, shortstop Manny Lee's offensive contributions were a far cry from the departed Fernandez.

The roster and team chemistry were the strongest since 1985 but the Jays still needed to improve. They won their third division title but were stunned 4–1 by the Minnesota Twins in the AL championship series. Still, there remained a sense that the Jays were on the way up after this playoff setback and the record 4,001,526 fans who came to SkyDome eagerly awaited the next season.

Roberto Alomar

STATISTICAL LEADERS

HOME RUNS	Joe Carter 33
RBIs	Joe Carter 108
BATTING AVERAGE	Roberto Alomar .295
STOLEN BASES	Roberto Alomar 53
WINS	Jimmy Key 16
ERA	Tom Henke 2.32
STRIKEOUTS	Duane Ward 132
SAVES	Tom Henke 32

HIGHS

◆ The Jays' starting rotation is buoyed by rookie pitcher Juan Guzman who posts an impressive 10–3 record and 2.99 ERA while Todd Stottlemyre enjoys his finest season with 15 wins.

◆ July 9 – A SkyDome record 52,382 spectators watches Jimmy Key get credit for a 4–2 win by the American League in the 62nd All-Star Game.

◆ The Jays become the first team in history to draw 4,000,000 fans.

◆ The Blue Jays defeat the California Angels 6–5 to claim their third division title.

◆ Joe Carter becomes the first player to drive in at least 100 runs three straight years with three different teams.

LOWS

◆ May 1 – at 44 years of age Nolan Ryan becomes the oldest pitcher to fire a no-hitter during a 3–0 win over the confounded Jays.

◆ Free agent signing Ken Dayley's season is ruined through injury; he makes only eight appearances and posts a 6.23 ERA.

◆ October 11, 1991 – In the crucial third game of the AL championship series the Jays hit a mere 3 for 16 with runners in scoring position, then lose 3–2 on a 10th-inning home run by Mike Pagliarulo off rookie Mike Timlin.

Snake Pits

1. Memorial Stadium, Baltimore 1977–83   (9–36)

The Jays did little right during their first seven years of travelling to Baltimore. Even when the team was competitive, their most heart-breaking series occured here when Tippy Martinez picked off three Toronto runners in the 11th inning of a key game.

2. Metropolitan Stadium, Minneapolis 1977–81   (5–20)

Before the Twins became more competitive themselves and moved to the Metrodome, the Jays couldn't buy a win in their old outdoor park. Three times Toronto failed to win even one game in a season on the road versus Minnesota.

3. Tropicana Field, Tampa 1998   (1–5)

The Jays saved some of their worst performances for the expansion Tampa Bay Devil Rays' home park. Toronto salvaged some pride by winning all six encounters between the two teams at SkyDome.

Tom Candiotti

4. Municipal Stadium, Cleveland 1977–81 (9–22)

The Indians were the second worst team in the AL East during this time and had no intention of being embarrassed at home even though few fans showed up for this "rivalry" anyway. In May 1981 Cleveland right-hander Len Barker threw a perfect game at the frustrated young Jays who dropped 14 of 17 here from 1979 to 1981.

Best Record

1. Fenway Park, Boston 1988–89 (13–0)

Despite wining the division in 1988, the Red Sox couldn't solve the Jays at Fenway. The following year an emotional sweep in Boston at the end of May was a catalyst in Toronto's improved play under Cito Gaston that led to the division championship.

2. Metrodome, Minneapolis 1982–87 (21–15)

While the Jays were a much improved team in the mid-eighties, they were also glad to rid themselves of Metropolitan Stadium. In 1984 they enjoyed their finest success at the Metrodome by winning five of six games.

John Olerud

3. Yankee Stadium, New York 1985–93 (39–20)

While the Jays fared reasonably well in the Bronx when they were a less successful club, they dominated the Yankees during this stretch of five division titles. Their most memorable series came late in 1985 when they took three of four from New York on the way to their first division title.

4. Kingdome, Seattle 1983–92 (40–20)

Toronto played .667 baseball on the road against their expansion cousins during this period of time. They also recorded a 36–24 mark against the Mariners at SkyDome for an overall 76–44 edge in wins.

Player Profile

Jimmy Key

Originally used by the Jays as a short reliever, Jimmy Key became one of the club's best starters and long-serving stars. His efficiency and coolness on the pitching mound earned him respect throughout the league. When he left the Jays after helping them win the 1992 World Series, he was among the club's all-time leaders with 116 regular season wins.

The quiet native of Huntsville, Alabama, received his first big break when both Stan Clarke and Bryan Clark experienced difficulties late in the pre-season. Key made the Jays' braintrust look good by saving ten games as a rookie in 1984 and setting a team record with 63 appearances. The following season he was shifted to the starting rotation where he won 14 games and helped Toronto capture its first division title.

The left-hander's key pitches included a superb curve ball and a fastball that he could run inside on right-handed hitters and away from those batting left. Key consistently reached double figures in wins including a career high 17 in 1987 which earned him a second place finish in the AL Cy Young Award voting after Roger Clemens. His consistency gave Toronto the crucial left-handed pitcher needed to become a legitimate contender.

Although he possessed a decent fastball, Key's location and control were crucial to his success. Only once did his ERA exceed 4.00 during his nine seasons with the Blue Jays. The veteran left-hander was on hand when Toronto won its first World Series in 1992. Following a brilliant performance in Toronto's 2–1 win over Atlanta in game 4 of the World Series, Key was given a long standing ovation by the SkyDome faithful. At this point it was no secret that Toronto was not going to re-sign him as a free agent; thus the long applause was an acknowledgement of nearly ten years' worth of excellent service. On this night Key also became the first Toronto starter to gain a win in the fall classic.

A few days later the popular lefty went out on a high note by entering game 6 in relief to earn the win as the Jays clinched their first ever World Series.

Key signed with the Yankees and pitched four years in the Bronx. In 1994 the Jays began their decline while Key started the all-star game. Two years later he was the winning pitcher in the decisive game of the World Series for the second time in his career as New York beat the Atlanta Braves. Key's next stop was Baltimore where shoulder woes finally ended his career in 1999. Overall, Key won nearly 200 games including twelve years of at least ten wins. After retiring he took to raising a family in rural Westchester County, New York.

Quotes

"My back hurts, my achilles hurts. I've been pounding Advil all day."
Nolan Ryan after tossing his record seventh no-hitter
versus the Blue Jays.

"Let them get all the attention; we can keep quiet and just win ball games."
Twins' closer Rick Aguilera after earning his third save
of the series to eliminate Toronto in five games.

AMERICAN 4, NATIONAL 2

National	ab	r	h	rbi	American				
Gwynn cf	4	1	2	0	R.Henderson lf	2	1	1	0
Butler cf	1	0	0	0	Carter lf	1	1	1	0
Sandberg 2b	3	0	1	0	Boggs 3b	2	1	1	0
Samuel 2b	1	0	1	0	Molitor 3b	0	0	0	0
Clark 1b	2	0	1	0	C.Ripken ss	3	1	2	3
Murray 1b	1	0	0	0	Guillen ss	0	0	0	0
Bonilla dh	4	0	2	1	Fielder 1b	3	0	0	0
Dawson rf	2	1	1	1	Palmer 1b	0	0	0	0
Jose rf	2	0	1	0	Tartabull dh	2	0	0	0
Calderon lf	2	0	1	0	Baines dh	1	0	0	1
O'Neill lf	2	0	0	0	D. Henderson rf	2	0	0	0
Sabo 3b	2	0	0	0	Sierra rf	2	0	0	0
Johnson 3b	2	0	0	0	Griffey Jr cf	3	0	2	0
Santiago c	3	0	0	0	Puckett cf	1	0	0	0
Biggio c	1	0	0	0	S. Alomar c	2	0	0	0
O.Smith ss	1	0	0	0	Fisk c	2	0	1	0
Larkin ss	1	0	0	0	R. Alomar 2b	4	0	0	0
Bell dh	1	0	0	0					
Totals	**35**	**2**	**10**	**2**	**Totals**	**30**	**4**	**8**	**4**

National	100	100	000 — 2
American	063	000	10x — 4

Molitor reached on catcher's interference.

E — Biggs. DP — American 2. LOB — National & American 8. 2B — Sandberg. HR — Ripken, Dawson. SB — Calderon. S — Guillen. SF — Baines.

	IP	H	R	ER	BB	SO
National						
Glavine	2	1	0	0	1	3
Harnisch	1	2	0	0	0	1
Smiley	0	1	1	1	0	0
Dibble	1	0	0	0	1	1
Morgan	1	0	0	0	0	1
American						
Morris	2	4	1	1	0	1
Key W	1	1	0	0	0	1
Clemens	1	1	1	1	0	0
McDowell	2	1	0	0	2	0
Reardon	2/3	1	0	0	0	0
Aguilera	1 1/3	2	0	0	0	3
Eckersley S	1	0	0	0	0	1

Smiley pitched to 2 batters in the 7th. IBB — off Dibble (Palmeiro). Umpires — Home, Brinkman (AL); First, McSherry (NL); Second, Kolser (AL); Third, Quick (NL); Left, Young (AL); Right, Banin (NL). T — 3:04. A — 52,383.

1992

96–66 .593 1st
Won World Series

The Season

The Blue Jays made history by becoming the first team from outside the United States to win the World Series. When Otis Nixon's bunt attempt was fielded by Mike Timlin and tossed to Joe Carter stationed at first base, the demons of 1985, 1989 and 1991 were exorcised. Toronto used sound pitching, explosive offence and team chemistry to waltz past the Oakland A's 4–2 in the AL championship series then the Atlanta Braves by the same count in the World Series.

Veteran Jack Morris was signed as a free agent to bring a winning attitude to the locker room and he responded with a team record 21 wins. Juan Guzman was the club's best starter with a 16–5 record and 2.64 ERA. Jimmy Key and Todd Stottlemyre also hit double figures in wins but it was the late season acquisition of David Cone that set the tone for the post-season. David Wells, Mike Timlin, Mark Eichhorn and Duane Ward all pitched well and the closing duties were in the reliable hands of Tom Henke.

The other important veteran signed by Toronto was outfielder Dave Winfield who contributed 108 RBIs, clubhouse leadership and the key hit that won game six of the World Series. The offence was also carried by Carter's 119 RBIs, White and Alomar's speed and power along with consistent production from White, Olerud, Maldonado and World Series MVP Pat Borders.

Two key home runs symbolized the Jays ascent to the status of playoff conquerers. In the ALCS, Alomar's blast off Oakland relief ace Dennis Eckersley tied game 4 at 6–6 after the Jays had trailed by five runs. This blast shifted the momentum decisively in Toronto's favour. In the World Series, the Jays dropped the first game but Ed Sprague's two-run pinch hit home run in the ninth inning of game 2 gave the Jays a 5–4 win and instilled the confidence that carried them to a six-game victory.

STATISTICAL LEADERS

HOME RUNS	Joe Carter 34
RBIs	Joe Carter 119
BATTING AVERAGE	Roberto Alomar .310
STOLEN BASES	Roberto Alomar 49
WINS	Jack Morris 21
ERA	Duane Ward 1.95
STRIKEOUTS	Juan Guzman 165
SAVES	Tom Henke 34

HIGHS

◆ April 6 – Jack Morris makes his major league record 13th consecutive opening day start and pitches the Jays to a 4–2 win over the Tigers.

◆ September 4 – The Jays tie an American League record with ten consecutive hits against the Minnesota Twins.

◆ September 24 – At 40 years of age, Dave Winfield becomes the oldest player in major league history to drive in 100 runs. Over all, he recorded 465 home runs and 1,833 RBIs in a stellar 22-year tenure. He entered the Baseball Hall of Fame in 2001.

◆ The Blue Jays become the sixth team, and the first since the 1943 St. Louis Cardinals, to go an entire season without being swept in a series.

◆ October 14 – the Blue Jays win their first American League pennant after trouncing the Oakland A's 9–2 in game six of the championship series.

◆ October 24 – the Blue Jays win their first World Series in a thrilling 4–3 win over the Atlanta Braves. Dave Winfield's two-out double in the 11th inning proves to be the difference.

LOWS

◆ Injuries continue to prevent left-hander Al Leiter from being a factor in the Jays' starting rotation. He only manages to appear in one game during the 1992 season.

◆ In an unfortunate mistake, the Canadian flag is brought out to the Fulton County Stadium field upside down prior to the start of the opening game of the World Series.

The Nine Clinching Games

October 5, 1985 — Toronto Blue Jays 5   New York Yankees 1
The night after blowing a ninth-inning lead and losing in extra innings, the Jays took control of this game from the start. Home runs from Moseby, Upshaw and Whitt combined with Doyle Alexander's complete game brought the Jays their first division crown.

September 30, 1989 — Toronto Blue Jays 4   Baltimore Orioles 3
The Jays won their second division title after beating back the challenge of a pesky Baltimore team that improved by 30 games in 1989.

October 2, 1991 — Toronto Blue Jays 6   California Angels 5
Toronto delighted the home crowd by clinching its third division crown with a come-from-behind victory over the Angels. Trailing 5–4

as they came to bat in the bottom of the ninth, the Jays rally was capped by Joe Carter's single which scored Roberto Alomar to send the club to the playoffs.

**October 3, 1992 — Toronto Blue Jays 3
Detroit Tigers 1**
Led by Juan Guzman's brilliant start, the Jays beat their old rivals to repeat as divison champions for the first time.

Juan Guzman

October 14, 1992 — Toronto Blue Jays 9   Oakland A's 2
The Jays won their first American League pennant by thrashing Oakland at SkyDome. Juan Guzman pitched seven strong innings while Joe Carter and Candy Maldonado hit key home runs.

October 24, 1992 — Toronto Blue Jays 4   Atlanta Braves 3

Dave Winfield's two-out double in the top of the eleventh inning provided the winning margin to bring the Jays their first World Series crown. Reliever Mike Timlin fielded Otis Nixon's bunt attempt and threw to Joe Carter at first base to seal the win.

September 27, 1993 — Toronto Blue Jays 2
Milwaukee Brewers 0

The reigning World Series titleists earned a chance to defend their crown when they clinched on the road for the first time at County Stadium.

October 12, 1993 — Toronto Blue Jays 6   Chicago White Sox 3

The Jays played their best baseball on the road in this series and clinched a second straight trip to the World Series at Comiskey Park. Veteran Dave Stewart pitched strongly and Devon White hit a home run to lead the Jays.

October 23, 1993 — Toronto Blue Jays 8
Philadelphia Phillies 6

On paper the Jays were superior to their opponents but the Phillies gave them all they could handle including the last game of the series. The Philles led 6–5 in the ninth inning when Joe Carter hit a three-run homer to keep the Jays on top of the baseball world.

Player Profile

Tom Henke

Standing 6'5" and hurling 98 mph fastballs past intimidated hitters, reliever Tom Henke was a fearsome sight to the opposition. This ability went all the way back to his days on the sandlot ball park in Taos, Missouri. In 1985 he was the compensation pool draftee added to the Jays when Cliff Johnson signed with the Texas Rangers as a free agent. The "terminator" developed into one of the game's top closers but the native of Kansas City, Missouri, was a laid-back and friendly individual off the pitcher's mound. Henke's consistency and coolness under pressure helped the Jays win four division titles and one World Series while he was with the team.

As Toronto entered the 1985 season, Bill Caudill was pencilled in as the closer. His inconsistency became a concern but in July Henke arrived from the minors to solidify the club's pitching. After posting three saves and three victories in his first six appearances, he finished with 13 saves as the club won its first division title and came within one game of reaching the World Series.

Between 1986 and 1992 Henke recorded over 200 saves and was the constant figure in the bullpen working with a succession of long relievers like Dennis Lamp, Mark Eichhorn and Duane Ward. He led the AL with 34 saves in 1987 and matched that total in 1992 when he helped the franchise win its first World Series.

The emergence of Ward as a potential closer as well as financial considerations allowed the Jays to let Henke go as a free agent. He signed with the Texas Rangers and saved a personal high 40 games in 1993. He retired two years later after one season with the St. Louis Cardinals. One of the top short relievers of his time, Henke finished with 311 saves and a career ERA of 2.67.

Quotes

"I really can't understand why no 40-year-old has done it before. Maybe everyone else retired and was playing with their grandchildren."

> Dave Winfield on becoming the oldest player
> to record a 100 RBI season.

"You know, I still think we should have won it all in '85. And I wish I had been able to contribute more this year. But I'm part of it and that's enough right now."

> Dave Stieb after the Jays defeated Oakland to
> qualify for their first World Series.

"You'll have to kill me not to start me."

> Jack Morris referring to the first game of the World Series.

"I didn't do a whole lot, but I did it at the right time."

> Dave Winfield after hitting the 11th-inning double that led the Jays
> to a World Series clinching win over Atlanta in game six.

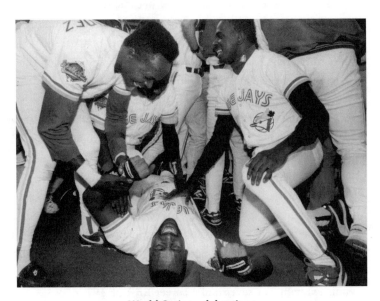

World Series celebrations

October 25, 1992

BLUE JAYS 4 at BRAVES 3

Game Six

Toronto	ab	r	h	rbi	bb	so	avg.
White cf	5	2	2	0	0	1	.231
RAlomar 2b	6	1	3	0	0	0	.208
Carter 1b	5	0	2	1	0	0	.273
Winfield rf	5	0	1	2	1	0	.227
Maldonado lf	6	1	2	1	0	0	.158
Gruber 3b	4	0	1	0	0	0	.105
Borders c	4	0	2	0	1	0	.450
Lee ss	4	0	1	0	0	1	.105
f-Tabler ph	1	0	0	0	0	0	.000
Griffin ss	0	0	0	0	0	0	—
Cone p	2	0	0	0	1	0	.500
Stottlemyre p	0	0	0	0	0	0	—
Wells p	0	0	0	0	0	0	—
c-DBell ph	1	0	0	0	0	0	.000
DWard p	0	0	0	0	0	0	—
Henke p	0	0	0	0	0	0	—
Key p	1	0	0	0	0	0	.000
Timlin p	0	0	0	0	0	0	—
Totals	**44**	**4**	**14**	**4**	**3**	**2**	

Atlanta	ab	r	h	rbi	bb	so	avg.
Nixon cf	6	0	2	1	0	0	.296
DSanders lf	3	1	2	0	0	0	.533
b-Gant ph-lf	2	0	0	0	0	0	.125
Pendleton 3b	4	0	1	1	0	2	.240
Justice rf	4	0	0	0	1	1	.158
Bream 1b	3	0	0	0	2	0	.200
Blauser ss	5	2	3	0	0	1	.250
Berryhill c	4	0	0	0	0	1	.091
1-Smoltz pr	0	0	0	0	0	0	.000
Lemke 2b	2	0	0	0	1	1	.211
d-LSmith ph	0	0	0	0	1	0	.167
Belliard 2b	0	0	0	0	0	0	—
Avery p	1	0	0	0	0	1	.000
PSmith p	1	0	0	0	0	1	.000
a-Treadway ph	1	0	0	0	0	0	.000
Stanton p	0	0	0	0	0	0	—
Wohlers p	0	0	0	0	0	0	—
e-Cabrera ph	1	0	0	0	0	0	.000
Leibrandt p	0	0	0	0	0	0	—
g-Hunter ph	1	0	0	1	0	0	.200
Totals	**38**	**3**	**8**	**3**	**5**	**8**	

Toronto	100	100	000	02 — 4	14	1	
Atlanta	001	000	001	01 — 3	8	1	

a-grounded out for P.Smith in the 7th. b-announced for Sanders in the 7th. c-grounded into fielder's choice for Wells in the 8th. d-walked for Lemke in the 9th. e-lined out for Wohlers in the 9th. f-lined out for Lee in the 10th. g-grounded out for Leibrandt in the 11th.

1-ran for Berryhill in the 11th.

E — Griffin (1), Justice (1). LOB — Toronto 13, Atlanta 10. 2B — Carter 2 (2), Winfield (1), Borders (3), DSanders (2). HR — Maldonado (1) off Avery. RBIs — Carter (3), Winfield 2 (3), Maldonado (2), Nixon (1), Pendleton (2), Hunter (1). SB — White (1), RAlomar (3), DSanders 2 (5). CS — Nixon (1). S — Gruber, Berryhill, Belliard. SF — Carter, Pendleton. GIDP — Cone.

Runners left in scoring position — Toronto 6 (Winfield 2, Maldonado 2, Gruber, DBell), Atlanta 6 (Nixon, Gant 2, Pendleton 2, Avery).
Runners moved up — RAlomar, Carter, Maldonado, Berryhill, Hunter.
DP — Atlanta 1 (Lemke, Blauser and Bream).

Toronto	ip	h	r	er	bb	so	np	era
Cone	6	4	1	1	3	6	103	3.48
Stottlemyre	2/3	1	0	0	0	1	11	0.00
Wells	1/3	0	0	0	0	0	4	0.00
DWard	1	0	0	0	1	1	16	0.00
Henke	1 1/3	2	1	1	1	0	33	2.70
Key W, 2-0	1 1/3	1	1	0	0	0	14	1.00
Timlin S, 1	1/3	0	0	0	0	0	2	0.00
Atlanta								
Avery	4	6	2	2	2	2	60	3.75
PSmith	3	3	0	0	0	0	39	0.00
Stanton	1 2/3	2	0	0	1	0	15	0.00
Wohlers	1/3	0	0	0	0	0	5	0.00
Leibrandt L, 0-1	2	3	2	2	0	0	35	9.00

Inherited runners scored — Wells 1-0, Timlin 1-0, Wohlers 1-0. IBB — off Stanton (Borders) 1. HBP — by Leibrandt (White). Umpires — Home, Shulock; First, Crawford; Second, Reilly; Third, West; Left, Morrison; Right, Davidson.

T — 4:07. A — 51,763.

1993

**95–67 .586 1st
Won World Series**

The Season

The Jays capped off an exciting year by becoming the first repeat World Series winners since the 1978 New York Yankees. They also became only the fourth club in history to emerge victorious in their first two trips to the fall classic. They won 95 games and enjoyed a seven-game cushion over the Bronx Bombers when the regular season ended. In the ALCS they swept the first two games over the Chicago White Sox in Comiskey Park before stumbling themselves in games three and four at the SkyDome. They recovered in time to post a 4–2 win and set up a World Series showdown with the Philadelphia Phillies. In a wild championship clash, the Jays won in six games after Joe Carter became the second player in history to hit a World Series-winning home run.

The daunting task of following up the 1992 World championship season was made more difficult by having to blend eleven new faces into the roster. Gone from the previous year's champions were key pitchers Tom Henke, Jimmy Key and David Cone as well as veteran Dave Stieb and young left-hander David Wells. In addition, Kelly Gruber, Candy Maldonado and Rance Mulliniks bid the club adieu. The void was filled by classy veterans Paul Molitor and Dave Stewart along with the emergence of Duane Ward as the top closer in the American League. The acronym "WAMCO" was respected throughout the league as Devon White, Roberto Alomar, Paul Molitor, Joe Carter and John Olerud represented the game's most feared upper and middle part of the batting order. Olerud,

Molitor and Alomar finished 1–2–3 in the batting race marking the first time this had happened since the 1891 Boston Reds. Late in the season the team did the unthinkable by trading for previous arch enemy Ricky Henderson to add more speed and experience to their drive to repeat. The perennial thorn in the Jays' side proved to be more of a psychological weapon as his numbers were unimpressive in the last quarter of the regular season and playoffs.

The team hit .279 and was led by AL batting champ John Olerud's .363 mark. The quiet first baseman and designated hitter made quite a bit of noise throughout the league by flirting with .400 until July. He was followed in the year-end batting race by teammates Roberto Alomar and Paul Molitor. Pat Hentgen, Juan Guzman and Todd Stottlemyre hit double figures in victories but Jack Morris fell from 21 to 7 wins. Al Leiter and Danny Cox proved to be decent fill-ins for Morris but this was a team built on offence and the stellar relief pitching of Duane Ward.

STATISTICAL LEADERS

HOME RUNS	Joe Carter 33
RBIs	Joe Carter 121
BATTING AVERAGE	John Olerud .363
STOLEN BASES	Roberto Alomar 55
WINS	Pat Hentgen 19
ERA	Duane Ward 2.13
STRIKEOUTS	Juan Guzman 194
SAVES	Duane Ward 45

HIGHS

◆ Trailing 6–5 in the bottom of the ninth inning in game six of the World Series, Joe Carter takes Phillies' reliever Mitch Williams over the wall to give the Blue Jays their second straight title.

◆ John Olerud bats .400 into August and ultimately wins the AL batting crown with a .363 mark.

◆ Pat Hentgen emerges as a bona fide star with 19 wins and 216 innings pitched.

◆ Dave Stewart and Paul Molitor prove to be excellent additions prior to the repeat season.

◆ John Olerud records 200 hits, 114 bases on balls and is hit by a pitch seven times while becoming the first Toronto player to reach base 300 times in one season.

LOWS

◆ After recording a team-record 21 wins in 1992, veteran right-hander Jack Morris posts a 7–12 record and an unsightly 6.19 ERA.

◆ Infielder Dick Schofield hits .191 in 36 games before losing the rest of the season to injury.

Most Frequent Trading Partners

1. New York Mets 8

Before inter-league play arrived, the Jays and Mets knew each other quite well. In their first exchange on December 12, 1980, reliever Roy Lee Jackson came to Toronto while the Jays sent their first-ever draft pick, Bob Bailor, to New York. While in the midst of two fierce pennant races, the Jays dealt with the Mets to pick up Mookie Wilson in 1989 and David Cone in 1992.

2. New York Yankees 7

Prior to the 1999 season, the Jays and Yankees pulled off a block-buster deal with pitchers Roger Clemens and David Wells as the principals. This was a much better return than the three nobodies

Dave Collins

Toronto received from the Bronx Bombers in return for David Cone on June 4, 1995. The Jays did get the better of New York in 1982 when the trading of journeyman reliever Dale Murray yielded future slugger Fred McGriff and veteran Dave Collins.

3. Atlanta Braves 7

In May 1986, the Jays rid themselves of unhappy starter Doyle Alexander in return for future ace reliever Duane Ward. This beneficial move helped to make up for the acqui-sition of the erratic Joey McLaughlin from Georgia in 1979.

4. Cleveland Indians 7

In 1976 the Jays made their first trade before they'd even played a game. They sent expansion selection Al Fitzmorris to the Cleveland Indians for catcher Alan Ashby. A month later they dialed the

Tribe's number again and came up with backstop Rick Cerone. Both these moves helped solidify the catching position for the team's infant years.

5. Texas Rangers 7

A month into their first season the Jays acquired Roy Howell from Texas, a move which bolstered their offence. In subsequent years they sent veterans Cliff Johnson and Candy Maldonado to the Rangers for prospects. On the eve of the 2000 season a three-way trade with Texas and Montreal brought former Expo Brad Fullmer to Toronto.

6. Oakland A's 6

Bitter rivals between 1989 and 1993, these two clubs completed a major trade in December 1984 which saw popular Jays Alfredo Griffin and Dave Collins sent west in exchange for "fireman" Bill Caudill. This trade was a bust but caused less commotion than the 1993 deal with Oakland that put Ricky Henderson in a Toronto uniform.

7. San Diego Padres 6

The Padres were the second team with which the Jays struck a deal when veteran reliever Jerry Johnson came to town in February 1977. On December 5, 1990, Toronto made probably its best trade thus far when key championship components Robert Alomar and Joe Carter were obtained from the Padres in exchange for Fred McGriff and Tony Fernandez.

Player Profile

Joe Carter

A feared power hitter and clutch performer, Joe Carter was crucial to the Blue Jays' success in the early 1990s. The talented outfielder came to Toronto from San Diego along with teammate Roberto Alomar. This transaction cost the team Fred McGriff and Tony Fernandez yet was probably the most important piece in the championship puzzle. Not only did Carter end the 1993 World Series with his dramatic ninth-inning home run, but he was also playing first base when Mike Timlin flipped Otis Nixon's failed bunt attempt to him to bring the club its first title the previous season.

Carter was a much-heralded prospect when the Chicago Cubs called him up for 23 games in 1983. The next season he was a key component of the package sent to the Cleveland Indians to obtain pitcher Rick Sutcliffe. Between 1984 and 1989, Carter topped the 30-home run mark twice and drove in more than 100 runs three times for the Tribe. He spent one year with the Padres before joining Toronto in December 1990. Carter was an immediate hit with the fans as he registered 33 home runs and 108 RBIs while helping the team win the AL East pennant in 1991. He was productive on the field and a team leader off it during the club's championship seasons in 1992 and 1993. Carter drove in at least 100 runs in six of his seven years in Toronto including the shortened strike season in 1994.

The gifted outfielder was a member of the Jays' feared "WAMCO" quintet in 1993 with Devon White, Roberto Alomar, Paul Molitor and John Olerud. Prior to the 1998 season he signed with the Baltimore Orioles but found himself added to the San Francisco Giants' pennant drive late in the year. Carter retired at the end of the season with 396 home runs and 1445 RBIs and the distinction of being the last Blue Jay involved in the play at the end of the 1992 and 1993 World Series wins. One of the most popular Blue Jays of all time, Carter remained in the public eye as a colour commentator on the club's television broadcasts until the end of the 2000 season.

Quotes

"It's easy for me to say John Olerud won't bat .400 because I think I know how tough it's going to be. He doesn't have a lot of speed. So he's not gonna beat out many infield singles."

Sparky Anderson

"I told my wife something really great was gonna happen tonight."

Joe Carter after hitting the World Series–winning home run versus the Phillies.

"The Blue Jays have set the standard, from the front office on down. They're the first team to have adapted to the conditions of the 1990s and have something to show for it."

ESPN broadcaster Joe Morgan

Molitor

Phillies 6 at Blue Jays 8
Game 6

Philadelphia	ab	r	h	rbi	bb	so	avg.
Len Dykstra cf	3	1	1	3	2	1	.348
Mariano Duncan dh	5	1	1	0	0	1	.345
John Kruk 1b	3	0	0	0	2	1	.348
Dave Hollins 3b	5	1	1	1	0	0	.261
Kim Batiste 3b	0	0	0	0	0	0	—
Darren Daulton c	4	1	1	0	1	0	.217
Jim Eisenreich rf	5	0	2	1	0	0	.231
Milt Thompson lf	3	0	0	0	0	0	.313
a-Pete Incaviglia ph-lf	0	0	0	1	0	0	.125
Kevin Stocker ss	3	1	0	0	1	1	.211
Mickey Morandini 2b	4	1	1	0	0	1	.200
Totals	**35**	**6**	**7**	**6**	**6**	**5**	

Toronto	ab	r	h	rbi	bb	so	avg.
Rickey Henderson lf	4	1	0	0	1	0	.227
Devon White cf	4	1	0	0	1	2	.292
Paul Molitor dh	5	3	3	2	0	0	.500
Joe Carter rf	4	1	1	4	0	0	.280
John Olerud 1b	3	1	1	0	1	0	.235
1-Alfredo Griffin pr-3b	0	0	0	0	0	0	—
Roberto Alomar 2b	4	1	3	1	0	0	.480
Tony Fernandez ss	3	0	0	0	0	1	.333
Ed Sprague 3b-1b	2	0	0	1	1	0	.067
Pat Borders c	4	0	2	0	0	0	.304
Totals	**33**	**8**	**10**	**8**	**4**	**3**	

Philadelphia	000	100	500 — 6 7	0
Toronto	300	110	003 — 8 10	2

One out when winning run scored.
a-hit sacrifice fly for Thompson in the 7th.
1-ran for Olerud in the 8th.
E — Alomar (2), Sprague (2). LOB — Philadelphia 9, Toronto 7. 2B — Daulton (2), Olerud (1), Alomar (2). 3B — Molitor (2). HR — Molitor (2) off Mulholland, Carter (2) off Williams, Dykstra (4) off Stewart. RBIs — Dykstra 3 (8), Hollins (2), Eisenreich (7), Incaviglia (1), Molitor 2 (8), Carter 4 (8), Alomar (6), Sprague (2). SB — Dykstra (4), Duncan (3). SF — Incaviglia, Carter, Sprague.
Runners left in scoring position — Philadelphia 4 (Kruk, Hollins 2, Stocker); Toronto 2 (Borders 2). Runners moved up — Alomar, Fernandez.

Philadelphia	ip	h	r	er	bb	so	np	era
Terry Mulholland	5	7	5	5	1	1	70	6.75
Roger Mason	2 1/3	1	0	0	0	2	27	1.17
David West	0	0	0	0	1	0	5	27.00
Larry Andersen	2/3	0	0	0	1	0	27	12.27
Mitch Williams L, 0-2	1/3	2	3	3	1	0	21	20.25

Toronto	ip	h	r	er	bb	so	np	era
Dave Stewart	6	4	4	4	4	2	120	6.75
Danny Cox	1/3	3	2	2	1	1	24	8.10
Al Leiter	1 2/3	0	0	0	1	2	21	7.71
Duane Ward W, 1-0	1	0	0	0	0	0	7	1.93

Stewart pitched to 3 batters in the 7th, West pitched to 1 batter in the 8th. Inherited runners scored — Andersen 1-0, Leiter 3-1. HBP — by Andersen (Fernandez). Umpires — Home, DeMuth; First, Phillips; Second, Runge; Third, Johnson; Left, Williams; Right, McClelland.
    T — 3:26. A — 52,195.

1994

55–60 .478 3rd

The Season

Before the players' strike ended the season and disappointed fans across North America in August, the Jays were in a difficult position. A number of injuries and sub-par performances undermined the club's attempt to "threepeat." Consequently, Toronto finished with a losing record for the first time since 1982. In a matter of months a transition took place from a championship calibre squad to a rebuilding phase.

The season began with little evidence of trouble as Joe Carter drove in a major league record 31 runs in April and rookie Carlos Delgado clubbed eight home runs over the same period. But the Jays could only muster 18 wins in May and June combined which effectively ruined their chances of reaching the post-season regardless of the labour situation. When the schedule came to an abrupt halt in August, Toronto sat sixteen games behind the front-running New York Yankees.

Pat Hentgen pitched well with 13 wins and a 3.40 ERA but Dave Stewart, Juan Guzman and Todd Stottlemyre faltered. The bullpen was devastated by the loss of closer Duane Ward and set-up man Danny Cox to season-ending injuries. Darren Hall compensated somewhat with an unexpected 17 saves but the team bullpen of Scott Brow, Greg Cadaret, Mike Timlin, Tony Castillo and veteran Dave Righetti was not enough to see the Jays through this difficult period.

Paul Molitor enjoyed a fine season at the plate and the performances of White, Alomar, Carter and Olerud were decent if not spectacular. The Jays' defence suffered from the lack of a stable line-up in the infield. Only Alomar at second base was a fixture. Ed Sprague's fielding at third was a liability, there was no constant figure at first base and neither veteran Dick Schofield nor young-sters Domingo Cedeno nor Alex Gonzalez made a consistent impact at shortstop. The overall batting average of the team slipped by ten points but the potential of young players like Delgado, Gon-zalez and Shawn Green offered promise.

STATISTICAL LEADERS

HOME RUNS	Joe Carter 27
RBIs	Joe Carter 103
BATTING AVERAGE	Paul Molitor .341
STOLEN BASES	Paul Molitor 20
WINS	Pat Hentgen 13
ERA	Tony Castillo 2.51
STRIKEOUTS	Pat Hentgen 147
SAVES	Darren Hall 17

HIGHS

◆ Rookie Carlos Delgado provides excitement in April by launching 8 home runs including a handful of tape measure shots.

◆ Joe Carter sets a major league record with 31 RBIs in April.

◆ August 4 – Joe Carter records his 100th RBI in only his 104th game, the fastest ever by a Toronto player.

◆ Paul Molitor enjoys a fine year by hitting .341 with 14 home runs and 75 RBIs while playing with the same gusto as the championship season.

LOWS

◆ The relief corps is devastated by the loss of Danny Cox after ten games and the inability of Duane Ward to play at all in 1994.

◆ Third baseman Ed Sprague fields poorly and puts up disappointing totals of .240 11–44.

◆ August 12 – players' strike suspends the 1994 season which is cancelled officially on September 14.

Players with the Most Home Runs in Their Only Season with the Blue Jays

1. Jose Canseco   46   1998

A Jays' tormentor when he starred for the Oakland A's, Canseco signed with the club in 1998 to help get his career back on track. He exploded for a personal best 46 home runs and combined with Carlos Delgado to set a team record for two players with 84 round trippers.

2. Dave Winfield   26   1992

Signed for his leadership as well as his presence at the plate, Winfield became the oldest player in league history to knock in at least

100 runs in a season. Later that year he drove in the World Series–clinching run for the Jays versus Atlanta.

3. Mike Stanley   22   1998

Stanley recorded 22 home runs in only 341 at bats before he was traded to Boston. He was part of a housecleaning undertaken by the Jays when they did not fare as well as anticipated in the standings.

Dave Winfield

4. Ron Fairly   19   1977

Fairly provided stability and experience in the Jays' young batting order during their inaugural season. His solid work was acknowledged when he was named the club's first-ever All-Star game representative.

5. Doug Rader   13   1977

Rader swung the bat well when he closed out his 11-year career by playing 96 games for the Jays in their first year. He retired with 155 home runs and 755 RBIs as a third baseman and designated hitter.

6. Jorge Orta 10 1983

Orta was acquired from the Mets as part of a continuing quest for a productive designated hitter. He was overshadowed by Cliff Johnson but still managed 10 home runs and 38 RBIs while helping the team enter the AL East pennant race for the first time. He was traded prior to the 1984 season to Kansas City for troubled slugger Willie Aikens.

Moseby with Bell and Barfield

Player Profile

Paul Molitor

Throughout his career, including three seasons in Toronto, Molitor was the quintessential line-drive hitter who epitomized professionalism. He was signed as a free agent by the Jays when they retooled for a run at a second straight World Series title in 1993. Molitor became part of the dreaded "WAMCO" batting arsenal with Devon White, Roberto Alomar, Joe Carter and John Olerud. The team won its second straight World Series and Molitor won accolades for his tenacity on the field and his sincerity off it.

The St. Paul, Minnesota, native spent fifteen years as one of the most popular Milwaukee Brewers of all time and helped the club reach the World Series in 1982. Able to play several positions, "Molly" was most comfortable at second base where his proficiency earned him a place in the starting line-up at the 1980 All-Star Game. Even when he was not operating at full capacity, the Brewers valued Molitor's natural eye at the plate and inserted him as the designated hitter. When his health returned, the DH spot was seen as a means of keeping the hard-playing Minnesota native from re-injuring himself.

Injuries often curtailed his playing time but, when healthy, his contribution was immense. In 1987 Molitor gained notoriety after recording a 39–game hitting streak. Eleven years after helping the Brewers win the American League pennant, he joined a talent-laden Jays' squad that won the World Series in 1993. Molitor hit .332 and recorded career highs of 22 home runs and 111 RBIs while earning his first World Series ring. After hitting .500 and driving in eight runs, he was chosen the most valuable player in the World Series. Molly's ability to hit to all areas of the field, his aggressive base running along with exemplary conduct off the field made him a role model for his younger teammates.

In 1994 and 1995 the Jays' fortunes sagged but Molitor continued to produce and compete with zeal. Prior to the 1996 season he went with his heart and signed with the Minnesota Twins. He played his last three years in the Gopher State and reached the 3,000 hit and 1,300 RBI milestones before retiring in 1998. He joined the Twins as a bench coach and resisted offers from the Jays to interview for the manager's position since he felt he lacked sufficient experience.

Quotes

"If it [the strike] does happen, nothin' much you can do about it."
Candy Maldonado commenting on the
impending end to the season.

"The players went out on strike when the average compensation was $1.2 million. All we want to know is, how much more do they want? We never get an answer to that question."
Owners' representative Richard Ravitch.

"All I can do is do the best I can and, as Pat said, things are in pretty good shape around here. I don't have a playing background as Pat did, I don't have a scouting background as Pat did, I don't have the on-field experience of some general managers. Player evaluations are not my strong suit. But I still feel capable of doing the job. There's going to be a lot of input from our scouting staff."
Jays' new vice-president and general
manager Gord Ash.

Roberto Alomar

April 5, 1994

White Sox 3 at Jays 7

Philadelphia	ab	r	h	rbi	bb	so	avg.
Raines lf	4	0	0	0	1	1	.000
Cora 2b	5	0	0	0	0	1	.000
Thomas 1b	4	1	2	0	1	0	.500
Franco dh	5	0	0	0	0	1	.000
Ventura 3b	2	0	1	0	2	0	.500
Dr Jackson rf	3	0	0	0	1	1	.000
LJohnson cf	4	0	2	1	0	0	.500
Karkovice c	4	2	2	1	0	1	.500
Guillen ss	4	0	2	1	0	0	.500
Totals	35	3	9	3	5	5	
Toronto	**ab**	**r**	**h**	**rbi**	**bb**	**so**	**avg.**
White cf	3	1	1	1	1	0	.333
RAlomar 2b	4	1	2	3	0	0	.500
Molitor dh	4	0	1	0	0	0	.250
Carter rf	3	1	0	0	1	0	.000
Olerud 1b	4	0	0	0	0	1	.000
Delgado lf	4	1	2	2	0	2	.500
Sprague 3b	3	1	1	1	1	1	.333
Borders c	3	1	3	0	0	0	1.000
1–Cedeno pr	0	1	0	0	0	0	—
Knorr c	1	0	0	0	0	0	.000
Gonzalez ss	3	0	0	0	0	2	.000
Totals	32	7	10	7	3	6	

Chicago	001 001 001 — 3	9	0
Toronto	001 000 33x — 7	10	0

1– ran for Borders in the 7th.

LOB — Chicago 10, Toronto 5. 2B — Thomas (1), Karkovice (1), Guillen (1), Borders 2 (2). HR — RAlomar (1) off McDowell, Delgado (1) off Cook, Sprague (1) off Cook, Karkovice (1) off Cadaret. RBIs — LJohnson (1), Karkovice (1), Guillen (1), White (1), RAlomar 3 (3), Delgado 2 (2), Sprague (1). SB — LJohnson (1). CS — RAlomar (1). S — Gonzalez. GIDP — LJohnson. DP — Toronto 1 (Cadaret, Gonzalez and Olerud).

Chicago	ip	h	r	er	bb	so	np	era
McDowell L,0-1	7	8	4	4	2	5	110	5.14
DeLeon	0	0	1	1	1	0	5	0.00
Cook	1	2	2	2	0	1	17	18.00
Toronto	**ip**	**h**	**r**	**er**	**bb**	**so**	**np**	**era**
Guzman W,1-0	7	7	2	2	3	4	117	2.57
Cadaret	1 2/3	2	1	1	1	1	33	5.40
Timlin	1/3	0	0	0	1	0	11	0.00

DeLeon pitched to 1 batter in the 8th. Inherited runners scored — Cook 1-1, Timlin 1-0. WP — McDowell, Guzman 2. Umpires — Home, Brinkman; First, Merrill; Second, Reilly; Third, Welke. T — 2:54. A — 50,484.

1995

56–88 .389 5th

The Season

The Jays finished a disappointing fifth in the shortened 144-game season. Spring training finished on a high note when the club reacquired pitcher David Cone from the Kansas City Royals. Once the season began, the team was unable to establish any momentum and, in late July, began to be disassembled when Cone was shipped to the division rival Yankees. In all, 20 pitchers appeared for the Blue Jays as they began to assess the quality of depth in the organization.

Despite the poor showing in the standings, many young players demonstrated an abundance of skill and potential. Right fielder Shawn Green hit 15 home runs and established a club rookie record with 50 extra base hits. Infielders Domingo Cedeno and Tomas Perez as well as catcher Sandy Martinez adjusted well to the rigours of the American League. Martinez's transition was particularly impressive as he hit .241 and played solidly behind the plate after making the jump from AA.

On the mound, lefty Al Leiter finally showed why the Jays sent Jesse Barfield to the Yankees to acquire him by posting an 11–11 mark despite a lack of consistent run support. Unfortunately Hentgen and Guzman struggled and, after the trading of Cone, the club lacked experienced starters. In the bullpen rookies Ken Robinson and Tim Crabtree were pleasant surprises and Tony Castillo pitched well as the closer. Overall, the pitching staff was in need of upgrading if the Jays were to improve upon the poor showing in 1995.

STATISTICAL LEADERS

HOME RUNS	Joe Carter 25
RBIs	Joe Carter 76
BATTING AVERAGE	Roberto Alomar .300
STOLEN BASES	Roberto Alomar 30
WINS	Al Leiter 11
ERA	Mike Timlin 2.14
STRIKEOUTS	Al Leiter 153
SAVES	Tony Castillo 13

HIGHS

◆ April 26 – The Jays pound the Oakland A's 13–1 in the home opener including a team record 11–run outburst in the second inning.

◆ July 29 – In the aftermath of the David Cone trade, the Jays faced the Oakland A's without a scheduled starter and minus second baseman Roberto Alomar who left the team for a day in protest. Rookie Giovanni Carrara steps in to earn the win, while Alex Gonzalez hits two home runs in a wild 18–11 victory.

◆ Shawn Green serves notice that he is the next Blue Jays star by pounding out a team rookie record 50 extra base hits while hitting .288 and demonstrating a fine arm.

LOWS

◆ July 28 – The Jays give up on the 1995 season by sending pitcher David Cone to the New York Yankees in exchange for young pitching prospects Marty Janzen, Jason Jarvis and Mike Gordon.

◆ October 1 – The Jays lose their fifth straight game to close out the season in last place for the first time since 1979.

Most Wins by a Pitcher the Year After Leaving the Jays

Jimmy Key

New York Yankees 1993   18 wins

The Jays chose not to re-sign Key after their World Series win in 1992 and he promptly won 35 games over two years for the Bronx Bombers. He also won 16 games for the Orioles in 1997 before arm problems ended his career.

Al Leiter

Florida Marlins 1996   16 wins

The Jays waited patiently for Leiter to reach his potential and stay injury free which he did in 1995. After the season he chose to sign with Florida and helped the team win the World Series in 1997.

Ken Schrom

Minnesota Twins 1983   15 wins

Schrom surprised everyone by recording a 15–8 season for the young Twins after winning a total of two games for Toronto in 1980 and 1982.

Pat Hentgen

St. Louis Cardinals 2000   15 wins

Hentgen was traded for reliever Lance Painter and catcher Albert Castillo to make way for young starters Chris Carpenter, Kelvim Escobar and Roy Halladay. He responded by matching the third highest win total of his career and helped the Cards win the National League central division title.

Todd Stottlemyre
Oakland A's 1995   14 wins
Stottlemyre left the Jays as a free agent and won 14 games for his
new club in 1995. He later won 14 and 12 games for St. Louis in
1996 and 1997.

Roger Clemens
New York Yankees 1999   14 wins
Coming off consecutive 20-win seasons in Toronto, Clemens' 14-10
mark was somewhat disappointing but this was offset by his first
World Series ring at the end of the season.

Doyle Alexander
Atlanta Braves 1987, Detroit Tigers 1987   14 wins
In his first full year after being traded from Toronto, Alexander went
9-0 down the stretch to help Detroit edge his old team in the 1987
pennant race.

Tom Underwood
New York Yankees 1980   13 wins
After pitching well but receiving little support in Toronto over two
seasons, Underwood registered a 13-9 record in the Bronx with the
eastern division champions.

Pete Vuckovich St. Louis Cardinals 1978 12 wins
After pitching effectively as a reliever and stater for the Jays in their
first year, Vuckovich went on to record three straight years of at
least ten wins for the Cards. In 1982 he won 18 games and the AL
Cy Young Award while helping Milwaukee reach the World Series.

Woody Williams San Diego Padres 1999 12 wins
Williams enjoyed his best year in the majors after the Jays
exchanged him for fellow starter Joey Hamilton prior to the 1999
season.

Player Profile

Roberto Alomar

Only those who followed the National League closely knew the budding star the Jays acquired along with Joe Carter from San Diego in December 1990. Alomar was a complete package of speed, hitting for average and power and superior fielding. Toronto parted with established stars Fred McGriff and Tony Fernandez to acquire Carter and Alomar. This key trade came at a time when the Jays were caught in a rut of only one division title over a five-year period when they were the most talented team in the AL East. Alomar became one of the greatest players to ever wear the Jays' uniform while helping the club finally reach its full potential.

Born in Ponce, Puerto Rico, Alomar hit .266 with 41 RBIs for San Diego in 1988. He continued to excel over the next two seasons and played in the 1990 All-Star game. After joining Toronto he took his game to a higher level and helped the Jays win three straight division titles and consecutive World Series in 1992 and 1993.

Beginning in 1992 Alomar hit at least .300 in four consecutive seasons and earned accolades as one of the greatest fielding second basemen of all time. His dramatic ninth-inning home run off Dennis Eckersley in game 4 of the 1992 AL championship series was the catalyst of Toronto's first World Championship.

Alomar soon grew restless as the Jays' fortunes sagged after their World Series win in 1993. His frustration culminated on July 28, 1995, when he left the club for 24 hours in protest following the trading of pitcher David Cone to the New York Yankees. Alomar signed with the Baltimore Orioles as a free agent prior to the 1996 season and played three years there before joining Cleveland in 1999.

Quotes

"It speaks of our commitment. It says we're not going to be retooling this year . . . that we're going to try and win."

Toronto GM Gord Ash after re-acquiring David Cone from
Kansas City just prior to the start of the season.

"I've already made a decision about whether to come back here or go for free agency. It [the David Cone trade] makes me think the Blue Jays are trying to rebuild. If you're a free agent, you have to go to a winning team."

Roberto Alomar after sitting out a game in late July after
David Cone was traded to the Yankees.

"I hope the players leave with the attitude that we all have to change. It starts with the off-season, not in spring training."

Joe Carter after the Jays' discouraging 5th-place finish.

"They had the chance to see me all year."

Roberto Alomar after sitting out the Jays' last game of the season and
denying the fans one last chance to see him in order to protect his
.300 batting average as he prepared for free agency.

July 30, 1995

A's 11 at Jays 18

Oakland	ab	r	h	rbi	bb	so	avg.
RHenderson lf	1	0	0	0	1	0	.287
b-Young ph-lf	2	1	1	1	2	1	.217
Gates 2b	6	0	2	4	0	0	.237
Giambi 3b	4	1	2	1	2	0	.237
Berroa dh	5	1	1	2	0	1	.267
Aldrete 1b	3	1	1	0	1	1	.264
Steinbach c	1	0	0	0	0	0	.260
GoWilliams ph-c	4	2	2	0	0	1	.375
Brosius rf	5	1	1	2	0	1	.246
Javier cf	3	2	2	1	1	0	.254
Bordick ss	3	1	1	0	0	0	.247
Paquette ss	1	1	0	0	1	0	.211
Totals	**38**	**11**	**13**	**11**	**8**	**5**	

Toronto	ab	r	h	rbi	bb	so	avg.
White cf	4	2	2	3	1	0	.304
AGonzalez ss	4	3	2	4	2	1	.246
Molitor dh	3	0	0	0	0	2	.241
?-Maldonado ph-dh	1	0	1	1	1	0	.260
Carter lf	5	1	1	0	1	1	.248
Olerud 1b	4	3	2	1	2	0	.258
Sprague 3b	4	3	2	1	0	0	.274
Green rf	4	3	3	2	1	0	.270
Parrish c	4	0	1	2	0	2	.194
Perez 2b	4	3	2	3	1	0	.211
Totals	**37**	**18**	**16**	**17**	**9**	**6**	
Oakland		000	500	501 — 11	13	0	
Toronto		075	200	22x — 18	16	0	

a-tripled for Steinbach in the 4th. b-walked for Henderson in the 4th.
?-doubled for Molitor in the 5th.

LOB — Oakland 10, Toronto 8. 2B — Giambi (2), Aldrete (7), Javier (9), Bordick (6), White (16), Maldonado (11), Olerud (19), Green 2 (20). 3B — GoWilliams (1). HR — AGonzalez 1 (7), off Prieto (8), off Woiciechowski, Perez (1), off Woiciechowski, Berroa (15), off Robinson, Brosius (7), off Carrara. RBIs — Young (5), Gates 4 (32), Giambi (12), Berroa 2 (52), Brosius 2 (22), Javier (26), White 3 (42), AGonzalez 4 (35), Maldonado (19), Olerud (30), Sprague (50), Green 2 (32), Parrish 2 (12), Perez 3 (4). SB — Javier (17). SF — Javier, Parrish. GIDP — Molitor. DP — Oakland 1 (Bordick, Gates and Aldrete); Toronto 1 (Perez).

Oakland	ip	h	r	er	bb	so	np	era
Prieto L, 1-4	2	7	9	9	2	2	51	4.08
Woiciechowski	1 1/3	5	5	5	1	1	37	6.55
Wengert	2	2	0	0	0	0	30	2.57
Briscoe	2/3	1	2	2	2	1	31	31.50
Mohler	2	1	2	2	4	2	55	4.91

Toronto	ip	h	r	er	bb	so	np	era
Carrara W, 1-0	5	7	5	5	5	2	100	9.00
Robinson	1 2/3	3	5	5	3	1	47	12.71
RJordan	1 1/3	1	0	0	0	2	24	5.00
Crabtree	1	2	1	1	0	0	10	2.25

Prieto pitched to 2 batters in the 3rd. Inherited runners-scored — Woiciechowski 2-2, Wengert 2-1, RJordan 3-2. HBP — by Briscoe (White), by Briscoe (Maldonado), by Prieto (Sprague), by RJordan (Aldrete). WP — Mahler. PB — Parrish. Umpires — Home, Martwether; First, Hendry; Second, Cobie; Third, Merrill. T — 3:31. A — 41,090 (50,516).

1996

74–88 .457 4th

The Season

The Jay's 20th-anniversary season was characterized by an 18-win improvement and a number of notable individual accomplishments. Key veterans rebounded into form and some vital younger players turned in strong seasons. Ultimately the team finished 18 games behind the World Series champion Yankees and seven in arrears of the wild card spot earned by the Baltimore Orioles.

Pat Hentgen became the first Blue Jays pitcher to win the Cy Young Award after posting a 20–10 record and 3.22 ERA. Juan Guzman returned to form with a league leading 2.93 ERA but, beyond the top two, the performances were spotty. Erik Hanson, Paul Quantrill, Marty Janzen, Woody Williams and veteran Frank Viola all struggled. The bullpen enjoyed a strong year with Mike Timlin's improved control and 31 saves leading the way. Tim Crabtree, Tony Castillo and Paul Spoljaric were a solid long relief trio.

There was sufficient power in the lineup with Ed Sprague, Joe Carter and Carlos Delgado combining for 91 home runs. Alex Gonzalez added 14 home runs and 64 RBIs to his stellar fielding while Jacob Brumfield and veteran catcher Charlie O'Brien contributed to the team's offensive depth. Rookie outfielder/DH Robert Perez showed poise at the plate with a .327 average in over 200 at bats. Overall the club lacked the depth of talent throughout the roster which characterized their strong showing from 1983 to 1993.

Rico Carty

STATISTICAL LEADERS

HOME RUNS	Ed Sprague 36
RBIs	Joe Carter 107
BATTING AVERAGE	Robert Perez .327
STOLEN BASES	Otis Nixon 54
WINS	Pat Hentgen 20
ERA	Tim Crabtree 2.54
STRIKEOUTS	Pat Hentgen 177
SAVES	Mike Timlin 31

HIGHS

◆ April 1 – The Jays begin their 20th regular season in Las Vegas with a 9–6 win over Oakland.

◆ April 9 – George Bell and Dave Stieb are the first two individuals placed in the club's "level of excellence."

◆ July 6 – Toronto records its biggest shutout win in franchise history by clobbering Detroit 15–0 at Tiger Stadium.

◆ November 12 – Pat Hentgen becomes the first Toronto pitcher to win the American League Cy Young Award.

LOWS

◆ After being signed away from division rival Boston, Erik Hanson disappoints with a 13–17 record and 5.41 ERA.

◆ Canadian Paul Quantrill struggles with his control and posts a dismal 5–14 record and ends up in the bullpen.

Most Career Home Runs When Joining the Jays

Dave Winfield 406

Winfield was a respected leader and feared hitter who appeared in twelve straight all-star games for the Padres and Yankees between 1977 and 1988. After signing as a free agent with the Jays, he helped them win their first World Series title in 1992.

Jose Canseco

Jose Canseco 351

Prior to hitting 46 home runs for the Jays in 1998, Canseco played with Oakland, Texas and Boston. He was best known for helping the A's win three straight AL West titles from 1988 to 1990 and the 1989 World Series.

Dave Parker 339

Parker joined the Jays for 13 games during the 1991 season after playing in Pittsburgh, Cincinnati, Oakland, Milwaukee and California. He was best known for winning the National League MVP award in 1978 and contributing to World Series titles in Pittsburgh in 1979 and in Oakland ten years later.

Willie Horton 285

Horton was a popular figure in Detroit for nearly 15 years and helped the club win the World Series in 1968. He joined Toronto briefly in 1978 before spending the last two of his 18 major league seasons with Seattle.

Jeff Burroughs 234

A former American League MVP, Burroughs was signed by Toronto in 1985 as the club continued to search for a reliable designated hitter. His production was lower than expected and the team was forced to re-acquire Cliff Johnson.

Ruben Sierra 234

During the prime of his career with Texas and Oakland, Sierra showed glimpses of superstardom but he was not able to excel consistently. In 1997 the Jays gave him a chance to help the club but he was released after hitting only .208 in 14 games.

Rickey Henderson 216

Henderson was added to the Jays late in 1993 as the Jays prepared to defend their World Series title; his influence proved more psychological than physical. His best years were spent with the A's and Yankees where he became baseball's all-time leader in stolen bases while recording four 20–home run seasons.

Al Oliver 214

A confident and talented batsman, Oliver shared DH and pinch hitting duties with Cliff Johnson when the Jays won their first division title in 1985. He was best known as a star on the Pittsburgh Pirates and Texas Rangers but also spent two years in Montreal where he won the NL batting title in 1982.

Ron Fairly 186

Fairly spent his 20th major league season by hitting a personal best 19 home runs for the Jays in 1977. A consistent fielder and hitter, he retired in 1978 with over 1,000 career RBIs.

Joe Carter 175

Carter joined Toronto in the blockbuster trade that also yielded star second baseman Roberto Alomar in December 1990. The hero of the 1993 World Series had already been a respected power hitter for six years in Cleveland and one in San Diego before joining the Jays.

Player Profile

Pat Hentgen

A hard-throwing right-hander with a good command of off-speed pitches as well, Pat Hentgen was one of the top pitchers developed in the Jays' system. His competitive zeal and loyalty to the organization were unmatched during his nine years in Toronto. He began on a high note with the World Series champions of 1992 and 1993 but remained fiercely devoted to the club when it declined between 1994 and 1996 before a trade to St. Louis severed his link to the team.

The native of Detroit, Michigan, honed his skills in the minors while waiting patiently for a chance to pitch on the Jays' deep roster. His opportunity came in 1993 when Jimmy Key left as a free agent and Jack Morris suffered through a poor season. Hentgen won 19 games and helped the club repeat as World Series champions. He showed tremendous poise for a young pitcher and signs of becoming an inspirational leader of the club's pitching corps.

Following a couple of average seasons in 1994 and 1995, Hentgen registered a 20–10 mark and won the American League Cy Young Award. The following year he won 15 games and played in his first all-star game. In both 1996 and 1997 he led or tied for the AL lead in complete games and shutouts. He also gained the respect of the Toronto fans for speaking out against the defection of many players at this time to other clubs as free agents.

After a 12-win season in 1998 and 11 wins in 1999, Hentgen was traded to the St. Louis Cardinals as the club made room for young starters Roy Halladay, Kelvim Escobar and Chris Carpenter. The veteran right-hander left the Jays as one of the most popular players in team history. Hentgen won 15 games in St. Louis and helped the team win the Central Division crown in 2000. Prior to the 2001 season, the former Toronto star returned to the AL East after signing with the Baltimore Orioles as a free agent.

Quotes

"I don't know if one person deserves it more than another, but if you look at the statistics, I'm right there in all of them. I'm just proud that my name will be beside that award forever."

> Pat Hentgen after becoming the first Toronto pitcher
> to win the AL Cy Young Award.

"He's a presence for this ball club and someone that we think is going to take us to the World Series this year."

> Jays' GM Gord Ash after signing Roger Clemens as a free agent.

"Believe me, the decision between Toronto and New York came down to a whisker – a whisker – and I think it was all about the kids at the stadium."

> Randy Hendricks, Roger Clemens' agent, referring to the
> Jays agreeing to allow Clemens to hit grounders to his
> sons a few hours before each home game.

"He sat on a chair in front of me and looked me right in the eye and said, 'They talk about Atlanta being the team of the 90s but did you know we sport one more world championship ring than they do?'"

> Roger Clemens describing Jays' president Paul Beeston's
> sales pitch when he began pursuing the former
> Red Sox ace as a free agent.

JAYS 9 at ATHLETICS 6

Toronto	ab	r	h	rbi	bb	so	avg.
Nixon cf	5	2	1	0	0	1	.200
Cedeno 2b	3	1	1	1	0	2	.333
b-Brito ph-2b	1	1	1	0	1	0	1.000
Carter lf	4	1	1	2	1	0	.250
Olerud dh	5	2	2	3	0	1	.400
Sprague 3b	4	0	0	0	1	3	.000
Delgado 1b	5	0	2	1	0	0	.400
Green rf	5	1	2	0	0	1	.400
AMartinez c	4	0	1	0	0	1	.250
AGonzalez ss	3	1	2	2	1	0	.667
Totals	**39**	**9**	**13**	**9**	**4**	**9**	
Oakland	**ab**	**r**	**h**	**rbi**	**bb**	**so**	**avg.**
Young cf	4	1	0	0	1	1	.000
Gates 2b	3	1	1	0	1	1	.333
Giambi 1b	3	1	1	1	1	1	.333
Berroa dh	4	1	1	3	0	1	.250
Plantier lf	2	0	0	0	2	0	.000
PMunoz rf	3	1	0	0	1	0	.000
Steinbach c	4	1	1	2	0	0	.250
Lovullo 3b	4	0	1	0	0	1	.250
Bordick ss	3	0	0	0	0	1	.000
b-Stairs ph	1	0	0	0	0	0	.000
Totals	**31**	**6**	**5**	**6**	**6**	**6**	

Toronto	100	140	030 — 9	13	0
Oakland	020	001	030 — 6	5	0

a-walked for Cedeno in the 7th. b-grounded out for Bordick in the 9th. LOB — Toronto 7, Oakland 4. 2B — Olerud (1), Gates (1). 3B — Carter (1). HR — Berroa (1) off Castillo; Steinbach (1) off Hanson; Cedeno (1) off Reyes; Olerud (1) off Reyes; AGonzalez (1) off Reyes. RBIs — Cedeno (1), Carter 2 (2), Olerud 3 (3), Delgado (1), AGonzalez 2 (2), Giambi (1), Berroa 3 (3), Steinbach 2 (2). SB — Nixon (1), Brito (1). CS — AGonzalez (1). GIDP — Berroa. DP — Toronto 1 (AGonzalez, Cedeno and Delgado).

Toronto	ip	h	r	er	bb	so	np	era
Hanson W,1-0	7	4	3	3	4	5	111	3.86
Castillo	1	1	3	3	2	0	21	27.00
Timlin S, 1	1	0	0	0	0	1	8	0.00
Oakland	**ip**	**h**	**r**	**er**	**bb**	**so**	**np**	**era**
Reyes L, 0-1	5	7	6	6	2	7	94	10.00
Mohler	1	2	0	0	0	0	22	0.00
Briscoe	2/3	0	0	0	2	0	17	0.00
Groom	1	3	3	3	0	0	21	27.00
Wengert	1 1/2	1	0	0	0	1	14	0.00

Inherited runners-scored — Groom 3-0, Wengert 2-2. Umpires — Home, Garcia; First, Voltoggio; Second, Reilly; Third, Craft. T — 3:02. A — 7,294 (47,313).

1997

76–86 .469 5th

The Season

Prior to the 1997 season the Blue Jays stunned the baseball world by signing free agent pitcher Roger Clemens from the Boston Red Sox. The main selling point was that Toronto's rebuilding had reached a point that a playoff position was a distinct possibility. The club behaved like a team fine tuning its roster by obtaining veterans Dan Plesac, Orlando Merced and Carlos Garcia from Pittsburgh. In reality the Jays were still a few years away from contending even though they had many positives.

Clemens did everything he could to get Toronto back into the post-season. He tied the club mark with 21 wins, posted a stingy 2.05 ERA and struck out a team record 292 batters on the way to winning his fourth Cy Young award. Pat Hentgen followed up his Cy Young season with 15 wins but after the top two there was little depth to the Toronto pitching staff. Woody Williams was an erractic 9–14 while Robert Person, Chris Carpenter and Juan Guzman all struggled. Person was particularly disappointing since the Jays thought enough of him to send John Olerud to the Mets in return. Paul Quantrill did well in long relief and rookie Kelvim Escobar showed flashes of excellence with 14 saves but generally the bullpen was unstable.

Delgado and Carter were the only consistent leaders on offence. Shawn Green hit 16 home runs but was still adjusting to the major leagues. Ed Sprague and Benito Santiago were shadows of their former selves and Alex Gonzalez's bat was not the equal of his glove. The July acquisition of budding star Jose Cruz Jr. helped kick-start the club and in the process they rid themselves of inconsistent pitchers Paul Spoljaric and Mike Timlin. Although he often lacked patience at the plate, the youngster hit 14 home runs in only 55 games and combined well with Green, Stewart and veteran Otis Nixon. In general it was felt that this team under-achieved and should have been closer than 22 games behind Baltimore.

STATISTICAL LEADERS

HOME RUNS	Carlos Delgado 30
RBIs	Joe Carter 102
BATTING AVERAGE	Shawn Green .287
STOLEN BASES	Alex Gonzalez 15
WINS	Roger Clemens 21
ERA	Paul Quantrill 1.94
STRIKEOUTS	Roger Clemens 292
SAVES	Kelvim Escobar 14

HIGHS

◆ June 2 – Roger Clemens is named AL pitcher of the month for May.

◆ June 30 – The Expos come to SkyDome for their first-ever regular season game versus the Jays.

◆ July 12 – Roger Clemens strikes out 16 Red Sox during an emotional return to Fenway Park.

◆ Carlos Delgado solidifies his position as an elite power hitter with his first 30-home run season.

◆ Roger Clemens posts a 21–7 record and is named the American League Cy Young Award winner.

LOWS

◆ September 10–22 – The Jays suffer through a disastrous 2–10 road trip against Oakland, Seattle, Boston and New York.

◆ September 24 – Cito Gaston is relieved of his managerial duties and replaced on an interim basis by pitching coach Mel Queen.

◆ In a year that began with such optimism, the Jays finish last in the American League East.

Best Toms

1. Tom Buskey

Journeyman Buskey spent his last three years in the majors in short relief for a weak Toronto club from 1978 to 1980. His best year was 1979 when he saved seven games while registering a 6–10 record and 3.43 ERA despite being on the worst Jays team of all time.

2. Tom Candiotti

While he only spent part of one season in Toronto, knuckleballer Candiotti solidified the starting rotation and helped the team win its third division title in 1991. His 2.98 ERA was the lowest of any of the Jays' regular starters.

Tom Underwood

3. Tom Underwood

Lefty Tom Underwood pitched better for the Jays than his 15–30 record indicated in 1978 and 1979. In 1978 he shared pitcher-of-the-year honours with Jim Clancy and won the honour outright the following season.

4. Tom Henke

Henke emerged as the Jays' closer in the second half of the 1985 season and was a key reason behind the club's first division title that year. The "terminator" went on to save a franchise record 217 games during his eight years in Toronto.

5. Tom Murphy

An experienced short relief specialist who recorded consecutive 20–save seasons for Milwaukee, Murphy provided experience and some quality work for Toronto from 1977 to 1979. He saved 11 games for the club while logging more than 200 innings over three seasons.

6. Tom Filer

In 1985 Filer came to the rescue with several quality starts when the Jays ran into a few nagging injuries. His 7–0 record and steady work helped the club maintain its hold on first place during a difficult stretch of the schedule.

Player Profile

Roger Clemens

The Jays stunned the baseball world when they signed former Red Sox ace Roger Clemens as a free agent on December 13, 1996. A native of Ohio, Clemens grew up in Houston where he starred in a number of high school sports before joining the University of Texas. He won the last game of the 1983 College World Series for the Longhorns before he was chosen by Boston in the first round of the major league amateur draft.

During thirteen seasons in Beantown, the hard throwing right-hander won at least 17 games six times, captured the Cy Young Award three times and helped his club reach the playoffs on four occasions. Although some questioned the status of his arm at the age of 34, Toronto general manager Gord Ash felt a change of scenery and the desire to prove Boston wrong would inspire Clemens to further greatness.

The Jays' latest big name star was supposed to combine with Pat Hentgen as the top starting tandem in the league and help lead the team back into the playoffs. Clemens lived up to all expectations but the club disappointed with a 76–86 record in 1997. Their marquee acquisition was often the lone bright spot in a frustrating year.

Clemens won 21 games and struck out a career high 292 batters in winning his fourth Cy Young Award.

In 1998 Toronto rebounded and remained in the wild card race for much of the season but ultimately lost out to the Red Sox. Clemens started slowly with a 5–6 record before reeling off a club record fifteen straight wins to register a 20–6 mark. For the second straight year he led all AL pitchers in wins, ERA and strikeouts and became the first pitcher to win five Cy Young Awards.

In the end Clemens was discouraged by Toronto's lack of progress in the standings and began hinting that he wanted out of the organization. On February 13, 1999, he was sent to the Yankees in a deal that yielded former Jays pitcher David Wells, reliever Graeme Lloyd and second baseman Homer Bush. All three were productive in 1999 while Wells and Bush remained keys to the club's fortunes in 2000. In New York, Clemens was not as dominant in the regular season as in the past but he was a key performer in the World Series triumphs of 1999 and 2000.

Quotes

"It's like driving down the road in a car with no steering wheel."
Otis Nixon after losing a fly ball in the twilight during the Expos–Jays series at SkyDome.

"Geez, when Roger started putting on a clinic from the second inning on, they [the fans] started standing when he'd get two strikes. You just don't ever see that for a visiting player."
Paul Quantrill after watching Roger Clemens strike out 16 Red Sox batters in an emotional return to Fenway Park.

"The only thing that's been tough on me is the way I've been treated . . . the things people say to me on may my out to the mound . . . kids throwing rocks at my car."
Cito Gaston after being relieved of his managerial duties.

Expos 2 at Jays 1

Montreal	ab	r	h	rbi	bb	so	avg.
Grudzielanek ss	3	1	1	0	0	0	.288
Lansing 2b	4	0	0	0	0	0	.275
Santangelo 3b	4	0	0	0	0	1	.313
Segui 1b	3	0	2	1	1	0	.327
HRodriguez lf	4	0	0	0	0	0	.280
Orsulak lf	0	0	0	0	0	0	.232
VGuerrero rf	4	1	2	1	0	0	.317
McGuire dh	3	0	0	0	0	1	.362
RWhite cf	3	0	0	0	0	0	.267
Widger c	3	0	1	0	0	1	.273
Totals	**31**	**2**	**6**	**2**	**1**	**3**	

Toronto	ab	r	h	rbi	bb	so	avg.
Nixon cf	4	0	1	0	0	3	.273
Merced dh	4	0	0	0	0	1	.282
Carter lf	4	0	0	0	0	3	.240
CDelgado 1b	2	1	1	1	1	0	.268
Sprague 3b	3	0	0	0	0	1	.250
SGreen rf	3	0	0	0	0	1	.271
BSantiago c	3	0	0	0	0	1	.195
AGonzalez ss	3	0	1	0	0	0	.248
CGarcia 2b	3	0	0	0	0	0	.209
Totals	**29**	**1**	**3**	**1**	**1**	**10**	

Montreal	010	001	000 — 2	6	0
Toronto	000	000	100 — 1	3	0

LOB — Montreal 4, Toronto2. 3B — Segui (2). HR — CDelgado (15) off PJMartinez; VGuerrero (4) off Hentgen. RBIs — Segui (29), VGuerrero (18), CDelgado (40). S — Grudzielanek. GIDP — HRodriguez, CGarcia. DP — Montreal 1 (Segui, Grudzielanek and Segui); Toronto 1 (CGarcia, AGonzalez and CDelgado).

Montreal	ip	h	r	er	bb	so	np	era
PJMrtnz W, 10-3	9	3	1	1	1	10	105	1.54

Toronto	ip	h	r	er	bb	so	np	era
Hentgen L, 8-5	9	6	2	2	1	3	99	3.11

Umpires — Home, Barrett; First, Roe; Second, Merrill; Third, Scott. T — 2:03. A — 37,430 (51,000).

Delgado collision

1998

88–74 .543 3rd

The Season

While the Yankees were running away from the rest of the league in 1998, the Blue Jays took a solid run at the wild card spot after recovering from yet another poor start. They seemed to settle down after deciding to go with young outfielders Shawn Green, Jose Cruz Jr. and Shannon Stewart on a full-time basis. Additionally, veteran Tony Fernandez stabilized the infield when he took over third base for the traded Ed Sprague.

Roger Clemens enjoyed another stellar year with a 20–6 mark and a second consecutive Cy Young Award. Pat Hentgen won 12 games but struggled with an ERA of 5.17. Juan Guzman's arm trouble caused the Jays to lose faith in him but Woody Williams and Chris Carpenter pitched well and combined for 22 victories. Veteran Randy Myers was traded despite 28 saves through the first week of August but Paul Quantrill, Dan Plesac and fireballer Robert Person combined for 17 saves. Dave Stieb made 19 relief appearances during an emotional comeback attempt going 1–2 with a 4.83 ERA as a long reliever and spot starter.

Signed as a free agent in the off-season, former rival Jose Canseco smacked 46 home runs as the DH and a very part-time outfielder. Carlos Delgado continued his ascent to stardom with 38 round trippers while Shawn Green became the newest Toronto hero with 35 home runs and 35 stolen bases.

Jose Cruz and Shannon Stewart appeared full of potential, combining for 23 home runs and 97 RBIs in less than a full season of work. Former Montreal Expo Darrin Fletcher was signed as a free agent and solidified matters at the catching position while the veteran Fernandez provided leadership on and off the field. The Blue Jays were blessed with much talent, proven and unproven. The main problem was convincing themselves and their fans that they were contenders in an era dominated by the division rival Yankees.

STATISTICAL LEADERS

HOME RUNS	Jose Canseco 46
RBIs	Carlos Delgado 115
BATTING AVERAGE	Tony Fernandez .321
STOLEN BASES	Shannon Stewart 51
WINS	Roger Clemens 20
ERA	Paul Quantrill 2.59
STRIKEOUTS	Roger Clemens 271
SAVES	Randy Myers 28

HIGHS

◆ July 1 – The Jays score eight times in the eighth inning during a come-from-behind 15–10 win over the New York Mets.

◆ July 4 – Tony Fernandez becomes the Jays' all-time leader with his 1,320th hit.

◆ July 5 – Roger Clemens becomes the 11th pitcher to record 3,000 strikeouts when he fans Randy Winn of the Tampa Bay Devil Rays.

◆ July 26 – Jose Canseco hits his 380th career home run to become the all-time leader among non-U.S. born players.

◆ August 25 – Roger Clemens sets a Jays record with 18 strikeouts during a 3–0 win over the Kansas City Royals.

LOWS

◆ July 31 – The Jays give up on Juan Guzman and trade the right-hander to the Baltimore Orioles for pitcher Nerio Rodriguez and outfielder Shannon Carter after he posts a disappointing 6–12 record.

◆ A late season rally is not enough to prevent the Jays from missing the post-season for the fifth straight year.

◆ Eric Hanson is ineffective in his last eleven games with the Blue Jays.

◆ Manager Tim Johnson's exaggerated war stories cause many to question his credibility in the Jays' clubhouse.

Memorable Games from Interleague Play

1. June 13, 1997   Carter returns to Philadelphia

To a loud chorus of boos World Series hero Joe Carter returned to Philadelphia's Veterans Stadium. Toronto lost its first ever interleague encounter 4–3 to the hometown Phillies.

2. June 30, 1997   Expos beat Jays (Martinez over Hentgen)

The historic first match-up between these Canadian cousins saw Montreal ace Pedro Martinez outduel Pat Hentgen in a thrilling 2–1 encounter.

3. July 1, 1997   Jays Versus Expos on Canada Day

The Expos won their second straight in front of the first sell-out at SkyDome since the 1995 home opener. Jeff Juden carried a no-hitter into the eighth inning of the 2–1 victory.

4. June 8, 1998   Marathon versus Marlins

The Jays lost 3–2 to Florida in a nailbiter that lasted 17 innings. This matched the Jays' longest game ever which first occured against Boston on October 4, 1980.

5. June 26, 1998   Return to Atlanta

The Jays defeated Atlanta 6–4 in the first game between the two clubs in that city since Toronto's World Series victory in 1992. Pat Hentgen outdueled John Smoltz to send his record to 9–4.

6. July 17, 2000   7–3 over Mets & Leiter

After struggling at home versus the Phillies, the Jays took it to the Mets and former teammate Al Leiter 7–3.

Player Profile

Carlos Delgado

Owner of a powerful swing and an above average glove at first base, Carlos Delgado became a bonafide American League star in the late 1990s. He was originally signed by the club as a free agent in October 1988. Delgado's beaming smile after launching one of his tape measure home runs became a common sight throughout the league by the 1996 season.

The native of Aguadilla, Puerto Rico, toiled in the Jays' minor league system before bursting out in 1992 and 1993 with consecutive 100–RBI seasons with Dunedin of the Florida State League and Knoxville of the Southern League. Fans in Toronto were treated to a glimpse of Delgado's future exploits when he hit eight home runs during the first month of the 1994 season. He was eventually returned to the club's top farm team in Syracuse to work on hitting off-speed pitches and being more selective at the plate. He gained a permanent place on the Toronto roster two years later.

In 1996 Delgado lived up to expectations throughout the entire season by hitting 25 home runs and 92 RBIs. This was followed up by his first 30-home run season and shoulder surgery that delayed his start to the 1998 schedule. The procedure was a success and Delgado went on to top all previous totals with 38 round trippers and 115 RBIs.

In 1999 he and Shawn Green both topped 40 home runs and kept the Blue Jays in the wild card race late into the season. Following Green's trade to the Dodgers prior to the 2000 season, Delgado's role as an offensive force and team leader was more important than in any previous season. He responded with 41 home runs, 137 RBIs and a .344 batting average and chased baseball's elite triple crown for most of the season. When the Jays became the first American League team to have four players hit at least 20 home runs at the All-Star break, Delgado led the way with 28.

Quotes

"I just told him that it happens to everybody and it probably won't be the last time it happens to him. It's not something that's easy to forget, especially with four days between starts."

> Pat Hentgen describing the advice he gave youngster
> Chris Carpenter after the latter was victimized for six runs
> in less than three innings versus the Atlanta Braves.

"The guys in the other league, talking to Greg Maddux, they tell me about getting over there but I don't know. I don't even want to take a guess at that. I've spent all my career in the American League obviously. You can think about that all you want but I've been pretty lucky to have done it here."

> Roger Clemens reflecting on his 3,000 career strikeouts
> in the more offensive-minded American League.

"I don't like the idea of helping Baltimore and Boston out."

> Jays reliever Dan Plesac on the trading of Juan Guzman to
> the Orioles and Mike Stanley to the Red Sox.

Royals 0 at Jays 3

Kansas City	ab	r	h	rbi	bb	so	avg.
Damon cf	4	0	0	0	0	3	.279
Sutton lf	4	0	1	0	0	2	.233
Offerman 2b	4	0	0	0	0	2	.312
Palmer 3b	3	0	1	0	0	1	.284
Pendleton dh	3	0	0	0	0	3	.246
Conine 1b	3	0	0	0	0	1	.256
Dye rf	3	0	1	0	0	1	.231
Fasano c	3	0	0	0	0	3	.219
LRivera ss	2	0	0	0	0	1	.247
a-HMorris ph	1	0	0	0	0	1	.313
Halter ss	0	0	0	0	0	0	.228
Totals	**30**	**0**	**3**	**0**	**0**	**18**	

Toronto	ab	r	h	rbi	bb	so	avg.
Stewart lf	4	0	0	0	0	0	.271
SGreen rf	4	1	2	0	0	1	.275
Canseco dh	3	0	0	0	1	0	.236
CDelgado 1b	3	0	0	0	0	1	.299
JoCruz cf	2	1	0	1	2	0	.260
TFernandez 3b	3	1	1	0	0	0	.305
Fletcher c	2	0	1	0	0	0	.278
Grebeck 2b	3	0	1	2	0	0	.267
AGonzalez ss	2	0	1	0	0	0	.249
Totals	**26**	**3**	**6**	**3**	**3**	**2**	

Kansas City	000	000	000 — 0	3	0
Toronto	100	000	20x — 3	6	0

a-struck out for Rivera in the 8th. LOB — Kansas City 3, Toronto 5. 2B — SGreen (25). RBIs — JoCruz (32), Grebeck 2 (18). S — AGonzalez. GIDP — TFernandez. DP — Kansas City 2 (Offerman, LRivera and Conine), (Dye and Conine).

Kansas City	ip	h	r	er	bb	so	np	era
Haney L, 5-6	6	5	3	3	3	0	96	7.17
Bones	1	1	0	0	0	1	11	3.60
Evans	1	0	0	0	0	1	11	1.04

Toronto	ip	h	r	er	bb	so	np	era
Clemens W16-6	9	3	0	0	0	18	130	2.76

Haney pitched to 3 batters in the 7th. Inherited runners-scored —Bones 3-2. HBP — by Haney (Fletcher), by Haney (CDelgado). Umpires — Home, Ford; First, Coble; Second, Hendry; Third, Young.
T — 2:16. A — 26,173 (51,000).

Paul Quantrill

1999

84–78 .519 3rd

The Season

Rather than build on their 88 wins in 1998, the Jays took a small step back in 1999 by posting a disappointing 84–78 record. During spring training the team rid itself of the distracting leadership of manager Tim Johnson and brought in Jim Fregosi. A few new faces in the line-up enjoyed solid seasons and the team's offence was among the league's best. One problem, however, was the lack of production from the DH position where a committee of batters turned an AL-low .249 average and surpassed only the paltry output of their counterparts in Detroit. Unfortunately the starting staff's ERA of 5.14 was far too high for the Jays to compete on a consistent basis during the heat of the wild card chase.

Prior to spring training, the Jays traded disgruntled veteran Roger Clemens to the Yankees. Unlike the David Cone transaction, this deal yielded players who could help immediately. David Wells became the ace of the starting rotation and responded with 17 wins while Homer Bush excelled as the first-string second baseman and Graeme Lloyd pitched well out of the bullpen. Kelvim Escobar completed his transition from short relief by winning 14 games while Chris Carpenter looked impressive at times. Veteran Pat Hentgen won 11 games and Roy Halladay posted an 8–7 record during his first big league season. Rookie closer Billy Koch saved 31 games and exhibited baffling movement on his blazing fastball.

The twin towers on offence were Shawn Green and Carlos Delgado. Both topped the 40–home run and 120–RBI levels and were complemented by newcomer Tony Batista's 22 round trippers after arriving in a trade with Arizona. Green caught the attention of the baseball world by registering a 28-game hitting streak during July. Shannon Stewart and Homer Bush combined for 69 steals while Darrin Fletcher and Tony Fernandez enjoyed productive RBI years. None of Dave Hollins, Willis Otanez or Willie Greene could hit with regularity while Jose Cruz continued to show a rookie's impatience at the plate. Overall the offence set team records with 883 runs scored and a .280 batting average. When the season ended, there was much optimism the Blue Jays could be a playoff calibre team if the pitching staff could improve in 2000.

STATISTICAL LEADERS

HOME RUNS	Carlos Delgado 44
RBIs	Carlos Delgado 134
BATTING AVERAGE	Tony Fernandez .328
STOLEN BASES	Shannon Stewart 37
WINS	David Wells 17
ERA	Paul Quantrill 3.33
STRIKEOUTS	David Wells 169
SAVES	Billy Koch 31

HIGHS

◆ Carlos Delgado and Shawn Green combine for 86 home runs and become the first Toronto duo to each hit at least 40 home runs in the same season.

◆ Tony Batista hits 26 home runs in 98 games after being acquired from the Arizona Diamondbacks.

◆ April 22 – The Jays complete a three-game sweep of the Anaheim Angels to begin the season 12–4.

◆ July 26 – The Jays beat the White Sox 4–3 in 11 innings for their ninth win in ten games.

◆ September 17 – Tony Fernandez sets a franchise record by playing in his 1,393rd game as a Blue Jay.

◆ October 2 – Billy Koch sets an American League rookie record with his 31st save as the Jays beat the Indians 7–3.

LOWS

◆ June 1 – the Jays lose 6–2 at home to the White Sox to fall to 24–29 on the season, 12–25 since their hot start.

◆ June 16 – Alex Gonzalez undergoes shoulder surgery and is lost for the season after getting off to the best start of his career.

◆ August 13–18 – In the heat of the wild card race, the Jays lose all six games of crucial home series against rivals Oakland and Texas.

The First and Last of the Millennium

Opponents:

Last: Cleveland Indians

First: Kansas City Royals

Sweep (at least 3 games):

Last: Detroit Tigers

First: Baltimore Orioles

Blue Jay Home Run:

Last: Jose Cruz Jr.

First: Shannon Stewart

Winning Pitcher:

Last: David Wells

First: Billy Koch

Billy Koch

Player Profile

Shawn Green

An impressive combination of speed and power, Shawn Green rose through the Jays' minor pro ranks between 1992 and 1994. During his first three pro seasons he displayed flashes of his potential but was still learning the nuances of the major league game. Between August 29 and September 12, 1995, he tied Alfredo Griffin's club rookie mark by putting together a 14–game hitting streak.

Green took his game to the next level in 1998 by hitting 35 home runs and stealing the same number of bases. The following year he topped the 40–home run mark and was selected to take part in the All-Star Game home run hitting contest. Green and Carlos Delgado were the most fearsome number three and four hitters in the league and kept the Jays in the wild card hunt for most of the season.

Despite his brilliance in 1998 and 1999, Green longed to play south of the border. There were also many observers who felt that he could play the game with more passion in general. When it became clear that he was not going to re-sign with Toronto, the club traded him to the Los Angeles Dodgers for Raul Mondesi and Pedro Borbon. Mondesi excelled for the Jays providing protection for Carlos Delgado in the batting order before his season was ended by an elbow injury. Green hit 24 home runs in his first Dodger season but the team failed to reach the post-season.

Quotes

"The unsettledness and the distractions had become the issue. It wasn't going to fade into the background as quickly as I hoped."

Gord Ash commenting on the dismissal of manager Tim Johnson prior to the start of the 1999 season.

"We feel like we wanted to make a change coaching-wise, to have some experience level on the coaching staff. It's got nothing to do with the coaches who are here. It's not a personal thing. Realistically, a manager needs people under him that he knows what they can do and is comfortable with."

Jim Fregosi explaining why coaches Mel Queen, Gary Matthews, Lloyd Moseby, Jim Let and Marty Pevey were dismissed at the end of the season.

"If you get caught up in pitching for some other people, you usually don't pitch that well. So, in my eyes, I've always pitched for my teammates and for myself."

Pat Hentgen after beating the Cleveland Indians 7–3 in what was his final game in a Toronto uniform.

Jays 7, Indians 3

Toronto	ab	r	h	rbi	bb	so	avg.
Bush 2b	6	1	2	0	0	1	.317
JoCruz lf	2	0	1	0	3	0	.238
SGreen rf	5	1	1	2	0	1	.312
Segui dh	3	1	2	0	1	0	.298
a-TFernandez ph-dh	1	0	1	0	0	0	.330
Fletcher c	5	1	1	0	0	0	.293
TBatista ss	5	1	2	3	0	1	.286
Otanez 1b	5	1	2	1	0	0	.236
CBlake 3b	5	1	1	1	0	1	.257
VWells cf	4	0	1	0	1	0	.262
Totals	**41**	**7**	**14**	**7**	**5**	**4**	

Cleveland	ab	r	h	rbi	bb	so	avg.
Lofton cf	5	0	0	0	0	0	.302
Vizquel ss	3	0	1	0	0	0	.331
EWilson ss	1	0	0	0	0	0	.262
RAlomar 2b	3	0	0	0	0	1	.323
Baerga 2b	1	1	1	0	0	0	.236
MRamirez rf	3	0	0	0	0	1	.335
ARamirez rf	1	0	1	2	0	0	.295
Thorne 1b	4	0	0	0	0	2	.277
Baines dh	2	0	1	0	1	1	.313
b-Cordero ph	0	1	0	0	1	0	.295
Justice lf	2	0	2	0	2	0	.287
Fryman 3b	2	0	0	0	0	1	.253
Houston 3b	1	0	0	0	0	1	.148
c-Sexson ph	1	0	1	1	0	0	.257
SAlomar c	4	0	1	0	0	0	.296
Totals	**33**	**3**	**8**	**3**	**4**	**7**	

Toronto	006	010	000 — 7	14	0
Cleveland	000	000	003 — 3	8	1

a-singled for Segui in the 8th. b-walked for Baines in the 9th. c-singled for Houston in the 9th.
E — Fryman (6). LOB — Toronto 12, Cleveland 7. 2B — Otanez (11). HR — ARamirez (3) off Hentgen; CBlake (1) off Brower; Otanez (7) off Wright; TBatista (25) off Wright; SGreen (42) off Wright. RBIs — SGreen 2 (123), TBatista 3 (75), Otanez (24), CBlake (1), ARamirez 2 (17), Sexson (116). SB — Vizquel (42). GIDP — SGreen, Fryman.
Runners left in scoring position — Toronto 6 (SGreen 2, Fletcher, Otanez, CBlake, VWells); Cleveland 4 (Lofton, EWilson, MRamirez, SAlomar).
Runners moved up — Fletcher, TBatista, RAlomar.
DP — Toronto 1 (TBatista, Bush and Otanez); Cleveland 1(EWilson, Baerga and Thorne).

Toronto	ip	h	r	er	bb	so	np	era
Hentgen W, 11-12	8	7	2	2	2	6	106	4.79
Lloyd	1/3	1	1	1	2	1	19	3.63
Koch S, 31	2/3	0	0	0	0	0	9	3.39

Cleveland	ip	h	r	er	bb	so	np	era
Wright L, 8-10	2 1/3	7	6	6	2	1	59	6.06
Brower	3 1/3	4	1	1	3	2	80	4.56
Karsay	1	2	0	0	0	0	13	2.97
Haney	1	1	0	0	0	0	23	4.69
MJackson	1	0	0	0	0	1	11	3.95

Hentgen pitched to 2 batters in the 9th.
Inherited runners-scored — Koch 2-0. Umpires — Home, Reed; First, Tschida; Second, Welke; Third, Iassogna.
T — 3:02. A — 43,049 (42,865).

Brad Fullmer

2000

83–79 .512 3rd

The Season

The Jays entered 2000 season with cautious optimism. Many players were on the verge of blossoming as top-notch big leaguers and the overall depth of the American League was not strong. The trading of Shawn Green to the Dodgers was not a popular move with the fans and there was concern that Raul Mondesi and Pedro Borbon would not offset this loss. While the Yankees remained the team to beat, they were ageing and did little to upgrade in the off-season. The Red Sox could count on ace Pedro Martinez every few days but little else. A playoff spot seemed within Toronto's grasp provided the young pitching staff settled in behind veteran David Wells and the offence lived up to its potential.

An enthusiastic crowd of 40,898 witnessed the Jays' 5–4 opening day victory over the Kansas City Royals. The club stumbled out of the gate, however, with a 4–9 record. The low point came during a three-game sweep at SkyDome at the hands of Seattle when the Jays were outscored 47–22. Critics pointed out manager Jim Fregosi's tendency to control all facets of the team as a major reason behind the lack of proper guidance being available to the club's youthful pitching corps. There was no shortage of offence as Carlos Delgado, Mondesi, newcomer Brad Fullmer, Tony Batista, Shannon Stewart, Darrin Fletcher and Jose Cruz Jr. all displayed power. The main problem was the poor performances of starters Chris Carpenter, Kelvim Escobar, Roy Halladay and Frank Castillo.

David Wells pitched well from the start but he was left on his own during the first month of the season. Escobar soon improved and Castillo developed into the team's second-best starter. The Jays jumped into first place for a few days during the last week of June but were unable to distance themselves from the Red Sox and Yankees.

Soon after the all-star break the Yankees caught fire while the Athletics took control of the wild card race. Toronto traded for starting pitchers Esteban Loaiza and Steve Trachsel along with veteran reliever Mark Guthrie, outfielder Dave Martinez and second baseman Mickey Morandini. A disastrous west coast road trip at the end of July wounded Toronto's playoff hopes.

On September 1 the Jays were purchased by Rogers Communications from Belgium-based Interbrew S.A. The transaction signalled a potential increase in broadcast revenue which would place the club in the category of "haves" within the current economic of baseball. A few days later a disappointing homestand against Oakland and Seattle dropped the Jays to $4\frac{1}{2}$ games out of the wild card spot. The team played well for much of the month but so did their rivals. A late season slump left the Jays out of the playoff picture for the seventh straight season.

STATISTICAL LEADERS

HOME RUNS	Carlos Delgado 41
RBIs	Carlos Delgado 137
BATTING AVERAGE	Carlos Delgado .344
STOLEN BASES	Raul Mondesi 22
WINS	David Wells 20
ERA	Billy Koch 2.63
STRIKEOUTS	David Wells 166
SAVES	Billy Koch 33

HIGHS

◆ April 3 – Shannon Stewart and Tony Batista become the 4th and 5th Toronto players to hit two home runs on opening day during the Jays' 5-4 win over Kansas City.

◆ May 8 – Jays set a new franchise record by hitting at least one home run in 19 consecutive games during 6-5 win over the Orioles.

◆ June 24 – The Jays move into first place by half a game following a 5-4 win at SkyDome over the Red Sox.

◆ July 9 – After Jose Cruz Jr. hits his 20th home run of the year, he joins Delgado, Mondesi and Batista, making the Jays the first team in AL history to have four 20-home run hitters before the All-Star break.

◆ July 11 – Sporting a 15-2 record, David Wells is the American League's starting pitcher in the All-Star game at Turner Field in Atlanta.

◆ September 8 – Brad Fullmer registers his 92nd RBI during a 3-0 win over Detroit to break Dave Winfield's team standard for a DH.

◆ September 17 – during a 13-1 romp over the White Sox, Carlos Delgado becomes the first Toronto player to record two 40-homer seasons.

LOWS

◆ A sparse crowd of 13,514 takes in the Jays' second game of the season.

◆ Seattle pounds Blue Jay pitching for 47 runs during an emphatic sweep at SkyDome.

◆ The Jays show signs of deteriorating by playing inconsistently against the Phillies and Mets to open the second half of the season.

◆ The Jays lose 23–1 in Baltimore to equal their greatest margin of defeat during a late-season slump that eliminates them from post-season contention.

Tom Henke

Best Canadian-Born Blue Jays

Paul Quantrill

Quantrill began his career as a long reliever for the Red Sox in 1992, then spent some time in the starting rotation the next season. He moved on to Philadelphia where he won a personal best 11 games in 1995 before the Jays acquired him prior to the next season. He struggled as a starter before finding his niche as a set-up man for such closers as Randy Myers, then Billy Koch.

Dave McKay

A solid and versatile player able to play three infield positions, McKay was picked up from the Twins by the expansion Jays in 1977. The Vancouver native was the team's starting third baseman on opening day that year and in 1978 enjoyed a 16–game hitting streak. He later played with Oakland and helped the team reach the AL championship series in 1981.

Rob Ducey

A native of Cambridge, Ontario, Ducey was a reserve outfielder for the Jays between 1987 and 1992. Occasionally he demonstrated impressive power and speed but the Jays were extremely deep in outfield talent at this time. He then moved on to California, Texas, Seattle and Philadelphia before Toronto re-acquired him briefly in 2000.

Paul Spoljaric

Kelowna, B.C., native Paul Spoljaric spent three years as a long reliever with the Jays where he demonstrated impressive velocity from the left side. In 1997 he was sent to Seattle as part of the package used to obtain Jose Cruz Jr.

Denis Boucher

A left-handed pitcher from Montreal, Boucher started seven games for Toronto in 1991 before he was traded to Cleveland as part of the payment for veteran Tom Candiotti. In 1993 he returned to his hometown to pitch for the Expos where he continued to show good control but lacked a legitimate fastball.

Rob & Rich Butler

These two brothers from the east end of Toronto both played the outfield. Rob was a useful reserve on the World Series team in 1993. He played one more year in Toronto before hitting .292 for Philadelphia in 1997. Rich joined the Jays in 1997 before joining Tampa Bay as a reserve outfielder the next year.

Player Profile

David Wells

Wells began his major league sojourn with the Blue Jays in 1987. During his first three seasons he was used almost exclusively as a left-handed long reliever before joining the starting rotation in 1990. In 1991 his 15 wins helped the Jays win their second eastern division crown in three years. When the Jays won their first World Series in 1992 they had so much pitching depth that Wells was moved back and forth between starting and relieving.

Seeking a more secure position in a starting rotation, Wells signed with the Detroit Tigers as a free agent in 1993 and won 26 games in $2^{1}/_{2}$ seasons. He pitched briefly with Cincinnati and Baltimore before joining the New York Yankees in 1997. Boomer contributed 34 wins to the Bronx Bombers' consecutive World Series titles in 1997 and 1998 and threw the century's 13th perfect game on May 17, 1998. He returned to his original club as the centrepiece of the package assembled by the Yankees to acquire the disgruntled Roger Clemens.

In his second stint in Toronto Wells proved to be every bit the dominant winner he was in New York. He led the Jays with 17 wins in 1999 and became the franchise's fourth 20–game winner in 2000 with a 20–8 mark. He was named as the starting pitcher in the 2000 All-Star Game and was the emotional pulse of the Jays' starting rotation. The respected veteran often took younger pitchers aside for encouragement and constructive help becoming, in effect, a player-coach.

Quotes

The offensive numbers "look like slo-pitch."
Former Toronto pitcher Jimmy Key's assessment
of the high scores prevalent in baseball.

"Really, coming out of spring training, he probably wouldn't have made the club if Joey Hamilton had been ready."
Manager Jim Fregosi reflecting on Frank Castillo's eighth
straight win to send his record to 9–5.

"We scored seven off Wells and weren't even close. That's tough."
Kansas City manager Tony Muser after a 15–7 loss to
the Jays on August 10.

"John can never have my information again. John knows it all. Let him figure it out. From now on, John Frascatore is a pitching coach for himself."
Pitching coach Dave Stewart commenting on the dugout
confrontation with John Frascatore during a game
in Texas on August 26.

Jays 6, Red Sox 4

Boston	ab	r	h	rbi	bb	so	avg.
Offerman 1b	5	0	0	0	0	0	.229
Frye 2b	4	1	1	0	0	0	.310
CEverett cf	3	1	2	1	1	0	.333
Garciaparra ss	4	1	2	2	0	0	.392
Daubach dh	4	0	0	0	0	3	.270
Varitek c	4	0	1	1	0	0	.285
DLewis rf	4	0	0	0	0	1	.265
Pride lf	2	0	0	0	1	1	.000
a-Hatteberg ph	1	0	0	0	0	1	.205
Alexander 3b	4	1	1	0	0	2	.224
Totals	**35**	**4**	**7**	**4**	**2**	**8**	

Toronto	ab	r	h	rbi	bb	so	avg.
Stewart lf	3	1	0	0	1	0	.349
ASGonzalez ss	2	3	2	2	0	0	.243
Woodward ss	1	0	0	0	0	1	.265
Mondesi rf	4	0	1	0	0	0	.277
CDelgado 1b	4	1	2	3	0	0	.359
Fullmer dh	4	1	1	1	0	0	.306
TBatista 3b	4	0	0	0	0	0	.277
JoCruz cf	4	0	2	0	0	0	.237
ACastillo c	4	0	1	0	0	0	.237
Bush 2b	3	0	0	0	0	0	.189
Totals	**33**	**6**	**9**	**6**	**1**	**1**	

Boston	011 000 020 — 4	7	1
Toronto	202 010 01x — 6	9	1

a-struck out for Pride in the 9th.

E — Garciaparra (8), TBatista (10). LOB — Boston 6, Toronto 5. HR — Fullmer (13) off Cormier; ASGonzalez (7) off Rose; Garciaparra (7) off Halladay; CDelgado (26) off Rose. RBIs — CEverett (68), Garciaparra 2 (39), Varitek (24), ASGonzalez 2 (30), CDelgado 3 (69), Fullmer (43). Runners left in scoring position — Boston 1 (Daubach); Toronto 2 (Stewart, TBaptista). Runners moved up — Frye, Garciaparra, Mondesi, ACastillo, Bush.
DP — Boston 1 (Offerman).

Boston	ip	h	r	er	bb	so	np	era
Rose L, 3-5	2²/₃	3	4	4	1	0	50	6.11
Pichardo	3¹/₃	4	1	1	0	0	34	2.25
Beck	1	0	0	0	0	1	6	0.00
Cormier	1	2	1	1	0	0	16	4.11

Toronto	ip	h	r	er	bb	so	np	era
Halladay W, 3-4	7	6	4	4	2	5	105	10.84
Quantrill	1	1	0	0	0	0	15	3.67
Koch S, 17	1	0	0	0	0	2	9	3.03

Halladay pitched to 2 batters in the 8th.

Inherited runners scored — Pichardo 1-0, Quantrill 2-2. HBP — by Rose (ASGonzalez). Umpires — Home, Hudson; First, Cederstrom; Second, Welke, Tim; Third, Scott.
T — 2:35. A — 30,130 (51,000).

2001

The 25th Season

The Season

The Blue Jays' 25th season coincides with the commencement of the Buck Martinez era. The Jays' newest manager was an exemplary defensive catcher who was also acclaimed for his ability to work with pitchers and contribute leadership in the club house. As a player, he is best remembered in Toronto as the right-handed hitting platoon with Ernie Whitt in the 1980s. In recent years his strong work as a commentator on Jays' television broadcasts has kept him in the public eye.

As the team prepares for the season opener against the Texas Rangers in Puerto Rico, a number of new faces and former Jays have been added to the mix. Left-handed reliever Dan Plesac returns to the Toronto bullpen after a fine season with Arizona in 2000. Right-hander Steve Parris was acquired from the Cincinnati Reds to enhance the club's pitching depth while Steve Frye was signed to add depth and experience at second base. Popular Jays Carlos Delgado, Darrin Fletcher and Alex Gonzalez were re-signed to provide talent and continuity on the field. The Jays started the New Year with a bang by sending disgruntled starter David Wells to the Chicago White Sox in exchange for 15-game winner Mike Sirotka, outfielder Brian Simmons and young pitchers Kevin Beirne and Mike Williams. As usual, the Yankees made a lot of noise in the off-season and this year they were joined by Texas. The Bronx Bombers aren't getting any younger and the Red Sox spent a heap of money on prototypical Boston player Manny Ramirez rather than add speed or pitching. The Jays are as good if not better than most AL teams and have a legitimate shot at the post-season as their first 25 years come to a close.

Anaheim Angels: (April 27, 28, 29)

Back in 1979, the California Angels thrashed the Jays 24–2 representing the low point of the Toronto club's worst season. Last year infielder Adam Kennedy lit up the Jays' pitching staff for eight RBIs during an April romp. The Angels are roughly at the same level as Toronto in that they are a talented club looking to improve their consistency and reach the post-season.

Atlanta Braves: (June 11, 12, 13)

Toronto defeated Atlanta twice in three games at SkyDome on the way to winning the World Series in 1992. Since inter-league play began there has been a healthy rivalry between the two although Atlanta has fared much better overall since the strike season in 1994.

Jose Cruz Jr.

Baltimore Orioles: (June 25, 26, 27, 28; August 3, 4, 5; September 18, 19, 20)

The Jays had the Orioles' number from 1999 to early in 2000 before their good fortune came to an end. Toronto bottomed out at the wrong end of a 23–1 score at Camden Yards in a late season slump that eliminated them from post-season contention. Over the years the Jays walloped the O's 24–10 at Exhibition Stadium in 1978 and locked horns with them in the 1983 and 1989 pennant races. Last year Cal Ripken became the 24th player to reach the 3,000 hit plateau. He embarks on his 21st season in 2001 where a place in the top 15 of baseball's all-time hit list is within reach.

Boston Red Sox: (May 31; June 1, 2, 3, June 29, 30; July 1, 2; July 18, 19)

The Red Sox have been a thorn in the side of the Jays of late. Three times, in 1986, 1988 and 1990, they won the AL East when Toronto underachieved. They also edged out Toronto in the battle for the wild card in 1999. Fenway Park was the sight of a key series in May 1989 which helped send the Jays on their way to winning the division in 1989. Boston was also the opponent in the infamous brawl of 1985 started by Bruce Kison hitting George Bell who responded with his karate kick.

Cleveland Indians: (September 14, 15, 16)

In the early days the Indians were clearly the second-worst team in the AL East after Toronto. The Jays often fared poorly against a Cleveland team that was determined to not look bad against their rivals for the division cellar. In subsequent years their development was the inverse of each other as the Jays were a powerhouse in the early 1990s while Cleveland became one of baseball's top outfits just as Toronto declined after the strike in 1994.

Chicago White Sox: (May 21, 23, 24)

Toronto and Chicago battled for the AL championship in 1993 when the Jays vanquished their opponent in six games. The White Sox were also the victims of Toronto's 9–5 onslaught in their inaugural game in 1977 and George Bell's extra-inning home run to close out the Exhibition Stadium era in 1989. Chicago slugger Frank Thomas enters the 2001 season on the verge of topping the 1,200 RBI mark for his career. The White Sox should draw a lot of attention this year since Boomer Wells will face his ex-mates while Mike Sirotka will be in the same position for the Jays.

Detroit Tigers: (August 31, September 1, 2)
Even though they now reside in the Central Division, the Tigers were Toronto's chief rival in the 1980s. In 1984 Detroit ran away with the division and ruined an excellent season by the Jays while in 1987 they upset a vastly superior Toronto club to steal the AL East pennant. Another component of this rivalry is the proximity of the two cities which has led to a number of Toronto fans making the trek to Motown for each series and a number of die-hard Tigers fans persisting in southwestern Ontario.

Florida Marlins: (June 8, 9, 10)
Although the 1997 World Series winners subsequently lost many players and dropped in the NL East standings, they became the most successful club in inter-league play. Last year in Miami, they hit consecutive ninth-inning home runs to stun the Jays and short reliever Billy Koch.

Kansas City Royals: (April 12, 13, 14, 15)
Everyone remembers the Jays coughing up a 3 games to 1 lead in the 1985 American League championship series versus Kansas City. Early in the Jays' history the Royals were kind enough to trade John Mayberry to Toronto. Last year Kansas City opened the season with a four-game set at SkyDome and battled hard to win the last two games and salvage a series split.

Minnesota Twins: (July 31, August 1, 2)

Although they've struggled lately as a small market team, the Twins won it all in 1987 and 1991. During their second World Series drive they victimized the favoured Jays easily in five games. The frustrating loss proved to be the the most valuable lesson of all for a Toronto team that went on to win the World Series in 1992 and 1993. Minnesota played the Jays tough in 2000 utilizing a pesky offence and bright young pitchers Eric Milton, Brad Radke and Mark Redman.

Montreal Expos: (July 6, 7 ,8)

The Expos and the Jays have enjoyed an intense rivalry since 1997. Last year Montreal ventured to SkyDome as a playoff contender with young stars Vladimir Guerrero and Jose Vidro. The Expos faltered in the second half but still offered some promise in 2001.

New York Yankees: (April 17, 18, 19, July 27, 28, 29; September 3, 4, 5)

The expansion Jays humiliated the Yankees on their own turf by a 19–3 count in September 1977. A few years later Toronto clinched their first AL East title in 1985 at the expense of the Bronx Bombers. In recent years New York has dominated Toronto in key games while enjoying a run of four World Series titles in five seasons. In 2001 the improved Jays will have their sights set on dethroning the Yankees as division champions.

Oakland Athletics: (May 8, 9, 10; August 14, 15, 16)

Between 1989 and 1992, Oakland and Toronto waged many epic battles on the baseball field. In 1989, the A's dominated the Jays in the AL championship series. Three years later Toronto gained revenge by dumping Oakland in six games on their way to winning their first World Series. During the 1999 and 2000 seasons the A's won key series at SkyDome which damaged Toronto's playoff chances. The defending West Division champions enter 2001 with one of the best young line-ups in baseball and a legitimate chance to dethrone the Yankees as World champions.

Seattle Mariners: (May 11, 12, 13)

The Mariners joined the major leagues along with Toronto in 1977 and initially fared better in the win column. A few years later their development stalled and the Jays became a league power. Finally in the mid-1990s Seattle developed its first bonafide contender and reached the AL championship series in 1995 and 2000. Last year they humiliated the Jays by scoring 47 runs in an early season sweep at SkyDome.

Tampa Bay Devil Rays: (April 9, 10, 11; June 5, 6, 7; September 21, 22, 23)

Since entering the league in 1998, the Devil Rays have proven to be frustrating at times for Toronto. That first year the Jays couldn't win in six tries at Tropicana Field. Last September, coming off a three-game sweep of the Yankees, Toronto fell flat against the Rays at SkyDome and took themselves out of the playoff race. Tampa Bay slugger Fred McGriff became the second player after Frank Robinson to hit 200 homers in each league and enters 2001 poised to pass the likes of Billy Williams and Dave Kingman on the all-time home run list. Tampa Bay will provide the opposition in the Jays 2001 home opener on April 9.

Texas Rangers: (April 24, 25; August 17, 18, 19)

Like most teams in the late 1970s and early 80s the Rangers feasted on the weak Jays. After Toronto lost Cliff Johnson to Texas as a free agent in 1984, they used the compensatory pick to claim Tom Henke who became one of the game's best closers. There has not been much of a rivalry between the two clubs but Texas did supply pitcher Esteban Loaiza to the Jays' stretch drive last year and boasts Canadian Jeff Zimmerman in their bullpen.

Jays' All-Time Standings
Excluding strike-shortened seasons
1981, 1994, 1995.

1985	99–62	.615	——
1992	96–66	.593	-3.5
1987	96–66	.593	-3.5
1993	95–67	.586	-4.5
1991	91–71	.562	-8.5
1989	89–73	.549	-10.5
1984	89–73	.549	-10.5
1983	89–73	.549	-10.5
1998	88–74	.543	-11.5
1988	87–75	.537	-12.5
1986	86–76	.531	-13.5
1990	86–76	.531	-13.5
1999	84–78	.519	-15.5
2000	83–79	.510	-16.5
1982	78–84	.481	-21.5
1997	76–86	.469	-23.5
1996	74–88	.457	-25.5

1980	67–95	.414	-32.5
1978	59–102	.356	-40.0
1977	54–107	.335	-45.0
1979	53–109	.327	-46.5

Quiz Questions

1. Which pitchers were credited with 2 wins each during the Jays' six-game World Series victory over the Atlanta Braves in 1992.

**(Jimmy Key — started and won game 4 won game 6 in relief,
Duane Ward — came on in relief and won games 2 and 3)**

2. Including the 2001 season, what club have the Jays faced most often in their season opener?

(Kansas City, 5 times — 78, 85, 88, 89)

3. Prior to the 2001 season, how many times have the Jays been alone or tied for first place at the All-Star Break?

(six — 83, 85, 91, 92, 93, 2000)

4. Who are the only two Jays pitchers to start the season with 11 straight wins?

**(Roger Clemens — 1997,
Dennis Lamp — 1985)**

5. When the Jays tied the AL record with 10 consecutive hits during an 8–run second inning outburst versus Minnesota on September 4, 1992, which player recorded the first and last hits of the inning?

(Kelly Gruber)